Exploring Digital Cultural Heritage

Exploring Digital Cultural Heritage

Access, Use, Value and Sustainability

Eirini Goudarouli, Anna-Maria Sichani
and Jane Winters

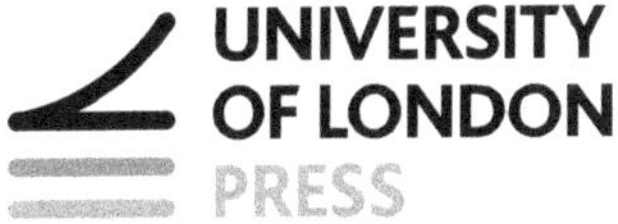

Available to purchase in print or download
for free at https://uolpress.co.uk

First published 2026 by
University of London Press
Senate House, Malet St, London WC1E 7HU

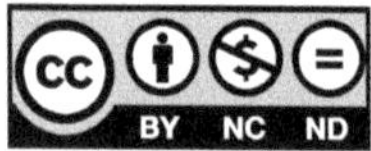

A CIP catalogue record for this book is available from The British Library.

ISBN 978-1-912250-94-3 (hardback)
ISBN 978-1-912250-95-0 (paperback)
ISBN 978-1-912250-98-1 (.epub)
ISBN 978-1-912250-97-4 (.pdf)
ISBN 978-1-912250-96-7 (.html)

DOI https://doi.org/10.63674/bxds6730

Cover image: Syuzann q/AdobeStock

Cover design for University of London Press by Nicky Borowiec.
Series design by Nicky Borowiec.
Book design by Nigel French.
Text set by Westchester Publishing Services, UK in Source Sans Pro, designed by Paul D. Hunt.

Contents

Abbreviations

AHRC	Arts and Humanities Research Council
API	application programming interface
BL	British Library
BVIM	balanced value impact model
CARE	collective benefit, authority to control, responsibility and ethics
CMS	content management system
CPF	Cultural Protection Fund
CRM	conceptual reference model
DIL	digital image licensing
DOI	digital object identifiers
ECHGS	Endangered Cultural Heritage in the Global South Hub
EUIPO	European Union Intellectual Property Office
FAIR	findable, accessible, interoperable, reusable
GLAMs	galleries, libraries, archives and museums
HTR	handwritten text recognition
ICA	International Council of Archives
IFLA	International Federation of Library Associations and Institutions
IIIF	International Image Interoperability Framework
LIBER	Association of European Research Libraries
LLMs	large language models
LOD	linked open data
MDS	Museum Data Service
ODA	Official Development Assistance
OOCWs	out-of-commerce works
PID	persistent identifier
POSI	principles of open scholarly infrastructure
SCCR	Standing Committee on Copyright and Related Rights
SNARC	Semantic Name Authority Repository Cymru
TNA	The National Archives, UK
UKRI	UK Research and Innovation

Series editors' preface

The Digital Cultural Heritage series is a forum for exploring the past, present and future of digital cultural heritage, both digitised and born-digital. This transdisciplinary, open access series of short-form books interrogates digital cultural heritage in all its forms, focusing on the key themes of use, access, value(s) and ephemerality. It considers histories of digitisation; the unequal and uneven heritagisation of new forms of cultural data; how individuals and institutions can adapt their practice and processes to exploit digital cultural heritage effectively; how digital cultural heritage is communicated to wider publics; skills for working with digital archives and collections; the politics and economics of digitisation; the values encoded in the digitised and born-digital; and how digital cultural heritage is embedded in teaching and learning practice.

One motivation for writing this volume has been to highlight some of the topics and ideas that we would like to see explored through future publications in the Digital Cultural Heritage series that this book initiates. It sketches out concepts and approaches that we hope will provide inspiration for formulating, discussing, challenging and rethinking a rapidly developing field of research and practice.

As editors of the series, we are most keen to hear in due course from authors and contributors working in geographical or thematic areas beyond our direct expertise and on the subjects and approaches that will shape studies in digital cultural heritage in the coming decades. For example, the majority of the initiatives and projects on which we draw in this book reflect the situation in the UK, drawing secondarily on European contexts. We acknowledge this focus on the Global North, which itself reflects an uneven and inequitable division of international resourcing and attention. To take a thematic example, we have not engaged in depth with the aesthetic and experiential dimensions of accessing digital cultural heritage, which are of such relevance for digital museology. There will inevitably be many other gaps and omissions.

The framing of the series is deliberately wide, concerned with digital cultural heritage wherever it may be located and by whomever it may be created. We hope that this book will be the beginning of a rich, diverse and informative debate that allows space for agreement, difference and development.

Eirini Goudarouli, Anna-Maria Sichani
and Jane Winters

Chapter 1

Introduction

Context

The aim of this book is to explore the multiple interpretations, contexts and uses of 'digital cultural heritage'. These elements will undoubtedly change over time – the concept of digital cultural heritage is still very much evolving – so this volume might best be described as a snapshot of a particular moment rather than any kind of definitive statement. Even if it necessarily delineates the present, however, we are just as much concerned with the pasts and possible futures of digital cultural heritage. The book is the beginning of what we hope will be an ongoing, critical discussion of what constitutes digital cultural heritage, who it is created by and for, the qualities that it shares with more traditional forms of cultural heritage (and those it does not), and what skills and values should be brought to bear when collecting, describing, displaying, exploring, analysing and preserving it. We hope that it will spark debate and conversation and bring our work into dialogue with other – perhaps contradictory – opinions and different forms of expertise and knowledge.

We are aware that there are different 'presents' depending on where an individual, community or institution happens to be located, and the resources and infrastructures that might be available to them. Consequently, we begin this book with a brief reflection on who we are as the authors of this book. We wish to consider, as far as we can, the experiences and assumptions that we bring to this research, and the knowledge that we both do and do not have. We have many things in common – we are all women who currently live in the United Kingdom – but have had different life and career trajectories. We come to this book from different standpoints, yet do not begin to capture all of the perspectives and skills that can be brought to bear when studying and working with digital cultural heritage. A historian of science by training, Eirini Goudarouli started her career holding research and managerial roles at the University Archives and the University Lab for the electronic processing of historical collections at the University of Athens in Greece. This early engagement with heritage collections and their digital representation, exploration and analysis led her to develop a passion for digital cultural heritage. In the UK she held various digital research roles in information-holding institutions and academia before she joined The National Archives, UK, where she is now the head of research. The current focus of her work is to drive innovation that enables the unlocking of physical, digital and born-digital collections in new ways, to broaden current understanding through ground-breaking interdisciplinary research and cross-sector collaborations. Anna-Maria Sichani is an interdisciplinary researcher, with a background in media and literary history and digital humanities. She started her international career with collaborations in crowdsourcing, digital cultural heritage projects and large-scale infrastructures in Greece, the Netherlands and the UK. Through a series of professional and community engagements, her interdisciplinary interests and expertise have come to centre on the development of sustainable knowledge infrastructures and communities of practice around open, reproducible, equitable and transparent data and software in the arts and humanities and cultural heritage. Her current work as a research associate in digital humanities at the School of Advanced Study, University of London, focuses on materiality, media changes and their entanglement with the digital, and on emerging computational methods, including their ethical and responsible development, for cultural heritage and research data. Finally, after a PhD in medieval history, Jane Winters began working in small-scale scholarly publishing at the Institute of Historical Research (IHR), University of London. Her first years at the IHR coincided with rapid advances in digital publishing and editing, and this led to her management of digital research and infrastructure projects like British History Online.[1] She is now professor of digital humanities in the School of Advanced Study, University of London, where she has a keen interest in both digital archives and infrastructure and open forms of digital publication. It is from these individual and collective vantage points that we begin to explore the complex world of digital cultural heritage.

The digital technologies of the late twentieth and early twenty-first centuries have had a transformative effect on research in the arts and humanities that engages with cultural heritage, and on research and practice in the cultural heritage sector. At the heart of this transformation has been the widespread digitisation of cultural heritage materials, creating machine-readable copies of text and image that can be accessed, analysed and manipulated in new ways and by new audiences (Jensen 2021; Owens and Padilla 2021). From initial experiments within Galleries, Libraries, Archives and Museums (GLAM) in the 1970s through to the mass digitisation of the 1990s and beyond, there is now an expectation that cultural heritage institutions, in the Global North at least, will 'host a proportion of their content online, and be engaging with the production of computer interactives' (Terras et al. 2021, 2). The consequences of this shift in modes of dissemination, access and knowledge creation remain emergent, but it is clear that 'mass digitization presents a new political cultural memory paradigm, one in which we see strands of technical and ideological continuities combine with new ideals and opportunities' (Thylstrup 2019, 4). The Council of Europe similarly records that 'Digitisation is profoundly changing our cultural experience, not only in terms of new technology-based access, production and dissemination, but also in terms of participation and creation, and learning and partaking in a knowledge society' (Council of Europe n.d., Understanding the Impact of Digitisation on Culture). In 2016, the UK Government published a Culture White Paper that set out the ambition to make 'the UK one of the world's leading countries for digitised public collections content. We want users to enjoy a seamless experience online, and have the chance to access particular collections in depth as well as search across all collections' (Department for Culture, Media and Sport 2016, 39); while in March 2018, the 'Culture Is Digital' policy paper recognised the power of digitisation to unlock cultural assets and the importance of making them more interoperable and discoverable (Department for Digital, Culture, Media and Sport 2018).

But this is not just a story of digitisation. Ever more of the world's cultural heritage is born digital, with no analogue referent. Traditionally, cultural heritage assets are physical items that are tangible and defined by their material characteristics (for example, paper, textile, wax) and can be preserved based on their aesthetic and physical qualities as well as their information value. If digitisation can tend to flatten out the differences between diverse forms of cultural heritage (for example, presenting manuscripts, books and newspapers alike by sheet, page or folio image), born-digital heritage is strikingly heterogeneous and multimodal. Born-digital heritage presents a landscape of new archival objects that come in a variety of formats (for example, Microsoft Word documents, emails, high-definition video, snapshots of websites and social media pages), with little or no structure, and require the existence of increasingly complex and flexible systems and rapidly evolving technological environments (Goudarouli 2023, 268). This raises unique preservation and access challenges, as well as licensing and copyright issues (and requires high levels of technical skill from both curator and researcher). The questions posed by new digital archives and collections are adding further layers of complexity and opportunity across sectors, bringing new challenges but also suggesting commonality of method and approach. Acknowledgement of the value of this new type of cultural heritage is apparent in the establishment of dedicated web archives in national GLAM institutions, and increasingly in the form of targeted funding, for example the major award to the HERMES project by the French government in 2024 (Ministère de l'Enseignement supérieur et de la Recherche 2024).[2]

The digitised and the born digital are often considered separately, and research into the born digital in particular can be highly specialised. Witness the development of new sub-fields of research such as web archive studies or critical web archive research (Ben-David 2021). Researchers and cultural heritage professionals, however, increasingly work across multiple digital and analogue formats. A contemporary historian studying the last decade of the twentieth century, for example, will find themselves working with printed, digitised and born-digital newspapers. An archivist or librarian accepting the personal 'papers' of an author will often be faced with a complex hybrid archive, consisting of handwritten material and typescripts but also hard drives, floppy disks and even downloaded social media data. A digital preservation specialist developing, implementing, maintaining and documenting digital preservation and access workflows and policies will often find themselves taking decisions about born-digital assets (for example, software, executable code, structured datasets and records derived from machine learning systems) that may influence the evolution of the digital infrastructures and archiving systems that support them. A museum curator planning an exhibition of video games will work with games in a variety of formats, an equally diverse range of hardware and the material culture of gaming magazines, arcades and user guides. It is our argument here that we should consider the digitalisation of cultural heritage as encompassing not just the digitised and the born digital but the structures and processes within which they are embedded.

Our understandings of digital cultural heritage need to be sufficiently broad to capture this diversity, while retaining the specialist knowledge and expertise that characterise work in GLAM institutions and with their digital collections. This tension is nicely highlighted by Prescott and Wiggins (2024) in relation to one of the four pillars of GLAM, that is, archives: 'As the boundaries of the archive continue to expand, there is a risk that the archive becomes a shorthand for all institutions of cultural memory, eliding museums, libraries, galleries, and archives under problematically unspecific and vague umbrella terms such as "cultural heritage", despite their distinct professional, theoretical, and institutional identities' (4). Both the digital and the analogue fall within this rather sceptical framing, even if we are only concerned here with the former. Prescott and Wiggins are right to be wary – 'umbrella terms' of this kind can serve to elide important differences in scope, remit and audience – but cultural heritage and its digital sibling have acquired a resonance, not least in relation to policy, that it would be unwise to ignore.

Nowhere is this more apparent than in the position statements, charters and other documents that set out the priorities for supranational organisations with an interest in access to and the preservation and exploitation of cultural heritage in its many forms. For example, in 2019 the European Commission stated that:

> Cultural heritage breathes a new life with digital technologies and the internet. The citizens have now unprecedented opportunities to access cultural material, while the institutions can reach out to broader audiences, engage new users and develop creative and accessible content for leisure and education. Europeana, for example, gives access to over 53 million items including image, text, sound, video and 3D material from the collections of over 3,700 libraries, archives, museums, galleries and audio-visual collections across Europe. (European Commission 2019, Europeana: Digitised Cultural Archives, with over 53 million items)

In 2021 the European Commission's updated Digital Cultural Heritage Policy recognised that 'Unprecedented opportunities brought by technologies, such as Data, AI, 3D and XR brings cultural heritage sites back to life . . . The transformation of the sector is resulting in easier online access to cultural material for everybody' (European Commission 2021). It also proposed a common European data space for cultural heritage, with the aim of accelerating the digitisation of cultural heritage assets. The proposed data space was added to Europeana, a well-established European digital cultural platform.

Among the most significant of the position statements produced by supranational organisations is the UNESCO Charter on the Preservation of the Digital Heritage, which was adopted at the thirty-second session of that body's General Conference in October 2003 (UNESCO 2009). The first article of the Charter defines digital heritage as consisting of:

> unique resources of human knowledge and expression. It embraces cultural, educational, scientific and administrative resources, as well as technical, legal, medical and other kinds of information created digitally, or converted into digital form from existing analogue resources. Where resources are 'born digital', there is no other format but the digital object. (UNESCO 2009, 1)

It goes on to describe what kinds of digital material fall within the scope of the definition: 'Digital materials include texts, databases, still and moving images, audio, graphics, software and web pages, among a wide and growing range of formats. They are frequently ephemeral, and require purposeful production, maintenance and management to be retained' (UNESCO 2009, 1). The Charter concludes by considering questions of access to digital heritage, the dangers of loss arising from the unique nature of digital materials, selection and preservation policies, and roles and responsibilities in relation to the safeguarding of digital heritage.

The role and influence of UNESCO in this sphere have been subject to critique. Fiona Cameron, for example, notes that 'Digital cultural heritage emerges as a result of a dialogue between UNESCO and heritage professionals. Through these dialogues, and by transposing heritage concepts onto digital resources, digital data became caught up in heritage procedures enmeshed in West-centred values' (Cameron 2021, 32). The broadness of the definitions and categories might also be challenged, but we would argue that it is in this very broadness that the value of the document lies. The digital landscape is continually evolving and it is impossible to predict the new forms of digital cultural heritage that may emerge in the next year let alone the next decade. In such an environment, over-specified policies and legal frameworks can be a hindrance to the vital work undertaken by GLAM institutions. Nowhere has this been more apparent than in the differing legislation that has enabled the creation of national web archives in Europe, a key type of born-digital cultural heritage. Just within the UK, what can be collected and, importantly, how it can be accessed differs between The National Archives, UK (TNA) and the British Library (BL). At TNA, government websites have been archived since 2003 under the terms of the Public Records Act, which were sufficiently broadly drawn as to require no change to accommodate born-digital data. Large-scale web harvesting at the BL, in contrast, required an extension to Legal Deposit before it could begin a decade later in 2013 (Winters 2020). Note, too, that responsibility for collecting this particular form of digital cultural heritage lies with two very different organisations, one a library and one an archive. Clear boundaries are not always possible, or even desirable, to maintain in relation to digital cultural heritage.

The UNESCO Charter talks of 'digital heritage', but in this volume we will use the term 'digital cultural heritage', foregrounding the cultural value of the digital. This cultural value, however, is neither universal nor universally expressed: 'The digital heritage is inherently unlimited by time, geography, culture or format. It is culture-specific, but potentially accessible to every person in the world. Minorities may speak to majorities, the individual to a global audience' (UNESCO 2009, 3). In a similar vein, 'heritage' is neither a uniform nor a static concept: its meaning and significance evolve over time and vary greatly among different communities and individuals. Yet, while early critical approaches tried to detach cultural heritage and memory from being a nation-state's instrument of 'imagined communities' (Anderson 1983) by introducing a more dynamic, culturally rich and collective framework for the ways through which people enable links with the past (Nora 1989; Assmann 2008), (digital) cultural heritage is still inextricably linked with memory politics and the politics of identity. Perhaps Stuart Hall's emblematic question 'Whose Heritage?' (Hall 1999) no longer has the same class or political connotations, but it remains of pressing importance among scholars in critical heritage studies focused on the tension between the concepts of 'universal heritage' and 'national heritage', especially in light of emerging nationalist and populist movements across the globe (Harrison, Dias and Kristiansen 2023), and even more emphatically in our networked era and in the case of digital cultural heritage. Dalbello reminds us, too, that digital cultural heritage has always existed outside the traditional sites of custodianship: 'right from the start, digital cultural heritage was localized in cultural communities of small reach and specialization, without much concern or awareness of a broader audience or scalable meanings; the hidden away, invisible, indistinct and intimate in contrast to public, visible, articulated and official' (Dalbello 2009, 5).

Memory and identity politics can thus explain why, although the UNESCO charter and its policies refer to a 'common' digital heritage and prioritise 'its preservation for the benefit of present and future generations [as] an urgent issue of worldwide concern', there are national variations in its application 'on the ground' (UNESCO 2009, 1): each country is responsible for safeguarding and preserving its own digital heritage through national cultural heritage organisations responsible for legal deposit, preservation and access to resources (Lusenet 2007; Cameron 2021). Indeed, there is no better place to trace these strong politics of identity than in national mass digitisation initiatives and the availability of corresponding funding, public or private, in cultural heritage institutions over the last twenty-five years (Terras 2022; Zaagsma 2023). At the same time, over the past decade, a series of international digital cultural heritage infrastructural repositories, such as Europeana, the Internet Archive and HathiTrust, have come to enhance national initiatives through the innovative linkage of dispersed digital cultural heritage collections (Benardou et al. 2019). These infrastructures are also linked from the outset to fragile international identities and Western-centric cultural policy agendas and come with a different set of embedded politics and biases (Thylstrup 2019; Kizhner et al. 2021; Capurro and Severo 2023).

On the other hand, 'heritage' is not simply frozen in time or solely connected to the past. Although cultural heritage institutions mainly preserve assets from the past that have already been assigned 'heritage status', in the case of digital and born-digital cultural heritage the main focus is towards what might be called 'living heritage' or more accurately 'heritage-to-be' (Lusenet 2007). This emphasis introduces a dynamic, evolving perspective on the concept of 'heritage'. The heritagisation of the present past (Butler 2006), especially in the case of born-digital cultural content, presents a historico-curatorial oxymoron as it is through the processes of selection, curation and digital preservation of that content that it is conceptualised as 'digital cultural heritage'. From this perspective, preservation is less about maintaining the past and more about anticipating what will be valued in the future and thus elevating contemporary born-digital cultural production to the status of 'future heritage'.

What precisely constitutes digital cultural heritage – what characteristics it does and does not share with more traditional forms of cultural heritage – is the subject of much research and debate. Taking the UNESCO Charter as a starting point, von Schorlemer notes:

> The specific characteristics of the digital heritage have led to its designation as a 'new heritage' in the literature. Features distinguishing it from analogue heritage include the possibility to copy digital objects an infinite number of times without a reduction in their quality . . . and its potential accessibility from everywhere in the world via the Internet. (Schorlemer 2020, 39)

Bonacchi and Krzyzanska have described heritage 'as the processes and outcomes of engaging with elements of the past – material and immaterial – and attributing social and cultural meanings to them in the present'. They go on to 'define the sub-field of digital heritage as examining interactions of this kind that are enabled by the Internet and the outcomes of such processes (the footprints – including data – that are produced)' (Bonacchi and Krzyzanska 2019, 1237). Münster and colleagues offer a rather simpler definition – 'digital heritage concentrates on tangible and intangible cultural heritage objects and their preservation, education and research' – but similarly identifies (im)materiality as a key consideration (Münster et al. 2019, 813).

Cameron and Kenderdine's important edited volume *Theorizing Digital Cultural Heritage* addresses 'digital cultural heritage as a political concept and practice', taking in such questions as

> the representation and interpretation of cultural heritage such as digital objects; issues of mobility and interactivity both for objects and consumers of digital heritage; the relations between communities and heritage institutions as mediated through technologies; the reshaping of social, cultural and political power in relation to cultural organizations made possible through communication technologies; and the visualization and interpretation of archaeological sites and historic environments. (Cameron and Kenderdine 2007, 2)

This approach is endorsed by McCrary (2011).

Cameron continues to adopt this expansive interpretation of digital cultural heritage but emphasises its tight connection with data: '*Digital cultural heritage* is conceived as all digital data that a society sees as important to retain and keep as a source of knowledge for future generations'. Of particular relevance for this volume, she distinguishes between two types of 'digital cultural heritage product': '*digitally born*, derived from data only existing in digital format, and *digital surrogates* (now popularly known as digitizations), or digital reproductions of pre-existing works' (Cameron 2021, 3–4).

Although the distinction between digitised and born-digital records remains valid and meaningful today, with each contributing to the expanding notion of digital cultural heritage, it is increasingly becoming a matter of degree rather than kind, particularly as we move towards more data-driven formats and processes. In practice, digitised and born-digital materials now coexist within shared digital infrastructures, face similar data-related preservation challenges and are encountered side by side in research, public engagement and institutional workflows. At the same time, the emergence of increasingly complex born-digital forms, such as immersive media, algorithmic art and AI-generated models and outputs, is radically reshaping our understanding of what constitutes cultural heritage. Digital cultural heritage should thus be seen less as a fixed field and more as a dynamic practice in constant motion and continual redefinition, a space that embraces and accommodates the unpredictable nature of technological and cultural change.

Themes and topics

All of these questions, concerns and considerations have informed the themes and topics addressed in this co-authored volume. In the following chapters, we will focus on four core thematic areas through which to consider digital cultural heritage: access, use and reuse, value(s) and sustainability. These themes cut across the digitised and the born-digital and are central to the work of the institutions responsible for the management and dissemination of digital cultural heritage and the researchers of all kinds who work with those digital materials. To an extent, this thematic division is an artificial one, and there will be intersection and some overlap in what follows, but it is one means of navigating a shifting and sometimes challenging landscape. The use of these themes also, we hope, helps to avoid the dangers of presentism that can afflict anyone who writes about digital technologies. So rather than discussing at length Artificial Intelligence (AI) and digital cultural heritage, which at the time of writing is the subject of much, often-polarised argument, we will address AI as just one aspect of use and reuse.

Turning first to questions of access, Chapter 2 will consider the influence and impact of open data in the cultural heritage sector, along with wider cultures of open knowledge and science. It will also explore the role of responsible and careful openness, which may involve limiting access to digital collections, or even closing them entirely. The ownership of digital cultural heritage will be discussed, including both activist, community and indigenous collections and the data held by the large commercial entities that are increasingly referred to and relied upon as archives. Finally, the impact of technological advances on access to digital collections will be explored.

Chapter 3, on use and reuse, tackles the thorny problem of copyright and licensing, which applies to all forms of cultural heritage but takes on a unique shape in the digital sphere. It addresses the loss of control that can occur when digital cultural heritage is placed in the public domain, in contrast to the stifling of innovation and creativity that can happen when institutions default to restrictive licensing practices. The chapter also begins to outline the skills and frameworks that enable work with digital cultural heritage, including technical expertise, but also effective documentation and ethical approaches that are both robust and adaptive. It concludes by introducing some of the tools and infrastructures that can both enable and constrain the use and reuse of digital cultural heritage.

In Chapter 4, we consider both the value of digital cultural heritage and the values that it encodes and represents. The question of value is highly relevant in relation to digital cultural heritage, as new kinds of objects and data stretch existing collecting policies and indeed infrastructures. To which forms of digital cultural heritage are value ascribed, and by whom? The chapter discusses which groups and individuals are represented in the digital materials collected by GLAMs and explores how the different forms of knowledge and contribution present in digital collections, large and small, are acknowledged and contextualised. It also considers how curators and users of digital cultural heritage can manage, and in some cases be protected from, challenging and even harmful materials.

Finally, Chapter 5 addresses the multilayered topic of preservation and sustainability. It explores practical considerations of preservation, the infrastructures needed to ensure that abundant digital cultural heritage is secured for the future, and concerns about data security and integrity. In addition to the physical infrastructures that are essential for sustainability, it examines the role of people, and particularly how communities outside GLAMs can be engaged with digital cultural heritage over the long term. Next, taking in a different facet of sustainability, it examines how cultural heritage institutions are thinking about the development of more environmentally sustainable digital preservation practices, which may ultimately lead to difficult decisions about when and what not to preserve and sustain.

In the conclusion, Chapter 6, we identify future areas for research and some of the topics and ideas that we would like to see given further consideration. These can only be suggestions rooted in a particular time and context, but we hope that they will serve as a jumping-off point for a rich and diverse debate that allows space for agreement, difference and development.

Notes

1 British History Online, a not-for-profit digital library, was launched in 2002 with funding from the Andrew W Mellon Foundation. It brings together primary and secondary source material for British history from the collections of libraries, archives, museums and academics. https://british-history.ac.uk [accessed 30 August 2024].

2 HERMES, one of six major investments in the humanities and social sciences, has three main objectives: 'structurer les capacités de recherche sur les patrimoines en devenir et développer un consortium interdisciplinaire avec une forte visibilité nationale et internationale, renforcer le transfert de la recherche vers les acteurs publics et la société, et favoriser une approche démocratique et inclusive du patrimoine culturel, en accord avec les besoins et les évolutions de la société' ('to structure research capabilities for heritage in the making and develop an interdisciplinary consortium with high national and international visibility, to strengthen the transfer of research to public actors and society, and to foster a democratic and inclusive approach to cultural heritage, in line with society's needs and evolution').

Chapter 2

Access

Opening up and accessing digital cultural heritage collections

Paul Koerbin issues a challenge for everyone concerned with the preservation of digital cultural heritage: 'Without access preservation is little more than a costly and meaningless storage burden' (Koerbin 2017, 195). This is, of course, a deliberate oversimplification; there are many kinds of cultural heritage – digital and otherwise – that cannot or should not be made accessible to everyone. Karolina Prażmowska, for example, notes that the digitisation of and access to Indigenous Peoples' Traditional Cultural Expressions 'can significantly increase opportunities for cultural appropriation and commodification of [their] cultural heritage' (Prażmowska 2020, 120). Archives spend considerable time trying to check for and remove sensitive or protected information from the digital materials that are deposited with or acquired by them, a process which becomes ever more difficult at scale (see, for example, The National Archives of the UK 2016). Without such sensitivity review, much archival material cannot responsibly be opened up for public access, or at least not without long periods of initial closure. But Koerbin does remind us of the important connection between the digital and expectations of access. The possibility of access to cultural heritage is greatly expanded when it takes digital form, and it is no longer necessary to visit an object, manuscript or collection in person to experience something of it. Certain kinds of born-digital cultural heritage, for example non-subscription websites, may always have been open and accessible to a global audience (although paradoxically they may become closed or subject to restricted access when archived) (Winters 2020).

Narratives around openness and access – of open access to knowledge – have long accompanied the growth of the digital. The formal concept of open access has been part of the research landscape for more than twenty years, with the Berlin Declaration on Open Access to Knowledge in the Sciences and Humanities serving as an important milestone in 2003. The language used is again strikingly wide ranging:

> Establishing open access as a worthwhile procedure ideally requires the active commitment of each and every individual producer of scientific knowledge and holder of cultural heritage. Open access contributions include original scientific research results, raw data and metadata, source materials, digital representations of pictorial and graphical materials and scholarly multimedia material. (Max-Planck-Gesellschaft 2003)

The Declaration is explicitly not only concerned with research produced in universities but also engages with cultural heritage and 'source materials' from the outset. Subsequently, discussions of open access, science and knowledge tended to be dominated by protocols around the sharing of the traditional outputs of scholarly research, for example journal articles. More recently, however, there has been a shift in attention to data, and it is here that digital cultural heritage once again comes into focus. Data means many things to many people, but for researchers and practitioners in the arts and humanities, it is primarily constituted from cultural heritage materials. An important concept here is the idea of collections as data, 'which raises the question of what it might mean to treat digitised and born digital collections as data rather than simple surrogates of physical objects or static representations of digital experience' (Padilla 2018, 296). The datafication of cultural heritage becomes possible when it is digitised or when its original form is digital.

Technological advancements towards opening up access

A key inflection point in relation to library and archival material was the advancement in technology that allowed projects and institutions not just to image documents and manuscripts but to make them machine readable through the application of Optical Character Recognition (OCR). A technology that is now routinely incorporated into smartphones transformed research using newspapers, printed books and pamphlets, the typed records of administration, and many other printed forms of expression. The title of an edited volume published in 2023 – *Digitised Newspapers: A New Eldorado for Historians?* – is redolent of the excitement that this has engendered for a very well-established and well-studied form of cultural heritage (Bunout, Ehrmann and Clavert 2023). A second inflection point is the recent maturity of Handwritten Text Recognition (HTR) software, which is opening up handwritten letters, books and manuscripts to analysis in a similar way. The widespread adoption of the Transkribus platform brings the benefits of datafication to the digitised cultural heritage of the medieval and early modern periods in particular.[1]

One of the earliest initiatives to experiment with HTR for historical document images was the tranScriptorium project, funded under the European Union's Seventh Framework Programme. It ran for three years from 1 January 2013 and tested its methods on two English-language corpora: the transcribed papers of the philosopher Jeremy Bentham (1748–1832), held at University College London; and the publicly available subset of Eighteenth Century Collections Online (Tanha, Romero and de Does 2013). The Bentham Papers were a key source as they had been the subject of a ground-breaking crowdsourcing project, Transcribe Bentham, in 2010–11. Crowdsourcing, described as 'a form of digitally-enabled participation that promises deeper, more engaged relationships with the public via meaningful tasks with cultural heritage collections' (Ridge et al. 2021), has been a key mechanism for opening up access not just to cultural heritage materials themselves but to the contexts within which they sit, the processes that lead to their publication and the narratives that are developed about them. Citizen scientists can transcribe, describe, annotate, enhance and even generate new cultural heritage data, for example by contributing their own memories and knowledge to collections. Crowdsourcing also serves to make cultural heritage more accessible even to those who do not participate directly in citizen science activities – or may not even know that their experience has been mediated by 'collective wisdom' (Ridge et al. 2021). The 'Tag along with Adler' project, for example, engaged volunteers (via the Zooniverse platform) to add their own tags to images from the collections at the Adler Planetarium in Chicago.[2] The aim was to capture the kinds of terms that non-specialists might search for rather than the more formalised language used in metadata created by museum staff and cataloguers, thereby making individual items in collections more discoverable – or discoverable in different ways (BrodeFrank 2024). Crowdsourcing is just one element of a more participatory culture that has developed in relation to cultural heritage, one which values different forms of knowledge and experience. Many aspects of this participatory culture have been enabled by digital technologies, and in particular the web and social media (see, for example, Giaccardi 2012).

The application of computer vision to digitised and born-digital cultural heritage materials seems likely to be the next technological means of transforming access, particularly to the object- and image-based collections held in museums and galleries (Liarokapis et al. 2020). The potential for enhanced search and linkage of industrial heritage collections, for example, has been explored by researchers in the Congruence Engine project, led by the UK's Science Museum Group.[3] The Heritage Weaver prototype aimed to draw connections within and between collections relying not on metadata or descriptive text but on machine-identified visual features and tropes (Kitcher et al. 2026). Brown (2024) notes the potential of computer vision to 'contribute meaningfully to object-based research . . . serving as a visual prosthetic that enables researchers to make feature comparisons across large bodies of work or that reveals qualities invisible to the human eye' (34).

Responsible and ethical open access

Access of this kind, and the research and understanding that it enables, relies on a culture of openness and sharing within the cultural heritage and academic sectors. Over the past decade, the Open Culture or OpenGLAM movement has emerged, encompassing cultural heritage organisations (GLAMs) that aim to provide 'ethical open access to cultural heritage' (OpenGLAM, n.d.-a). OpenGLAM brings some of the concepts and values of the broader open access movement to the cultural heritage sector and there were early attempts to position the activity of mass digitisation as increasing access to cultural and heritage content in line with the objectives of the open access movement (Terras 2015). The OpenGLAM movement was first spearheaded in Europe in the early 2010s by institutions like the Rijksmuseum, which aimed to make its online collections freely accessible. Over the past decade, and with contributions from members of the Creative Commons community, the Wikimedia Foundation and the Open Knowledge Foundation, OpenGLAM efforts have grown significantly, with numerous institutions and individuals across the globe providing frameworks, pilot studies and use-cases in order to define policies, approaches and practices for opening up access to their digital collections. The OpenGLAM community drafted the OpenGLAM Principles (OpenGLAM, n.d.-b) and at the time of writing is co-developing a 'Declaration on Open Access for Cultural Heritage' to guide more equitable practices around open access in digital cultural heritage.[4] In order to operationalise all of this work, over the last decade, GLAM Labs (under the various names they have adopted) have been set up within many cultural heritage institutions as 'in-house' drivers for the implementation of enhanced access to and reuse of cultural heritage data. They operate at the intersection of digital cultural heritage, research, innovation, technology and creativity (Mahey et al. 2019) and have been vital in driving experimentation and collaboration. They have seeded ideas and indicated important directions of travel, but their work has all too rarely come to influence business-as-usual within under-resourced institutions (Winters et al. 2022).

The process of making cultural heritage data publicly accessible often has a significant technological element, including the need to ensure data is machine-readable and structured in a way that allows it to be linked with other datasets. A concept closely linked to open data in cultural heritage is that of the 'FAIR principles' (Findable, Accessible, Interoperable, Reusable), originally introduced in 2016 to provide guidelines to the scientific community for research data management and stewardship (Wilkinson et al. 2016). The cultural heritage community has widely embraced the FAIR principles, as they offer a valuable framework for assessing and digitally publishing cultural heritage data in order to improve discovery, ensure sustainable access and promote better sharing and reuse (Koster and Woutersen-Windhouwer 2018). Given that the FAIR principles refer to data, metadata and infrastructure (GO FAIR, n.d.), three types of entities that are heavily used within digital cultural heritage, compliance with them has become a baseline requirement in digital cultural heritage projects and infrastructures. It has also, however, opened up a field of enquiry concerned with the ongoing technical challenges of how to implement FAIR data sustainably (Hermon and Niccolucci 2021).

If openness is broadly to be welcomed as a precondition for greater access, the CARE Principles for Indigenous Data Governance remind us that it cannot always be the default: 'greater data sharing alone creates a tension for Indigenous Peoples who are also asserting greater control over the application and use of Indigenous data and Indigenous Knowledge for collective benefit' (Carroll et al. 2020, Abstract). The CARE Principles

– Collective Benefit, Authority to Control, Responsibility and Ethics – are designed to ensure that Indigenous communities are able to assert greater control over how Indigenous data held by cultural heritage institutions and other bodies is used and accessed (Carroll et al. 2020; 2021). While the FAIR principles offer a data-centric approach, the CARE principles are people- and purpose-oriented, 'reflecting the crucial role of data in advancing innovation, governance, and self-determination among Indigenous people' (Carroll et al. 2020, Abstract). The goal is that stewards and other users of Indigenous data will 'be FAIR and CARE', embracing both sets of principles in all aspects of their data work (Carroll et al. 2021). Along the same lines, the Principles of Open Scholarly Infrastructure (POSI) underline the importance of open infrastructure. POSI offers a set of sixteen principles across three themes (Governance, Sustainability, Insurance) by which open scholarly infrastructure organisations and initiatives that support the research community can be run and sustained.[5]

Access for a fee

In contrast to the growing culture of responsible and ethical openness that is being promoted within the cultural heritage and knowledge sectors, much of the world's digital cultural heritage is controlled by commercial entities. This commercial interest first became apparent in relation to the mass digitisation that began in the mid-1990s. A Jisc report published a decade or so after the first investments in digitising cultural heritage at scale noted that, in the UK alone, 'a conservative estimate suggests £130 million of public money has been spent on the creation of digital content since the mid-1990s' (Jisc 2005, 2). But it was not just public money that was being spent; commercial publishers often partnered with GLAMs to digitise and make available their collections. Thylstrup notes that this 'integration of commercial platforms into the otherwise primarily public institutional set-up of cultural memory . . . produced a reconfiguration of the political landscape of cultural memory' (Thylstrup 2019, 5). The consequences have been profound and connect to all four of the values that lie at the heart of this book. There is, of course, a trade-off between availability of any kind, however restricted, and open access. Nor are the financial barriers to access uniform. Public interest in genealogy and family history has driven significant digitisation in the UK and elsewhere and companies like Ancestry and FindMyPast have enabled access to vast historical collections for people who do not have the benefit of institutional support for research.[6] At the time of writing, FindMyPast advertises that it hosts 'more than 10 billion genealogy records, including the 1921 census' – all yours for £24.49 a month (or £169.99 a year). The commodification of digital cultural heritage is apparent here not just in the subscription but in the reference to 'genealogy records' rather than collections or primary sources (we will return to this in Chapter 3, 'Use and Reuse'). A different kind of partnership is apparent in the relationship between GLAMS and digital publishers, whose target market is not family historians but higher education institutions. Companies like Gale (part of Cengage Learning) and ProQuest invested significantly in the digitisation of important historical collections, with a business model that relies on high levels of (costly) institutional subscription. They are, and should be expected to act like, businesses, but locking cultural heritage behind a paywall does inevitably constrain access. It also determines the kinds of cultural heritage that will be digitised, that is, the material for which there is a market.

Commercial imperatives are also in play for born-digital cultural heritage, with potentially more serious consequences for access – and particularly for continuity of access. Material posted on the web and social media is an important form of cultural heritage. There are numerous institutions and initiatives concerned with the archiving and preservation of the web, whether globally (the Internet Archive's Wayback Machine) or nationally (for example, national libraries such as the Bibliothèque nationale de France and the British Library), but platform-based social media content is far more of a challenge.[7] The value of this material, and of persistent access to it, is increasingly recognised (see, for example, Rees 2021; Wallenius 2022; Schafer and Pailler 2024), but there are numerous, sometimes insuperable, barriers to access for both institutions and individuals. A complex web of legal deposit regulation, platform terms of use, data protection legislation and technical hurdles faces those wishing to archive and make available social media (Cannelli 2024). Social media platforms are not, of course, archives and access to their content can be curtailed for commercial or other reasons at little or no notice. The closure of once-important services, and the subsequent loss of unique cultural heritage, is a fact of twenty-first-century life. Nowhere was this more starkly illustrated than by the removal of free access to the Application Programming Interface (API) for the social media platform that was then called Twitter (now X). The relative ease of access to Twitter data had allowed the development of a lively ecosystem of tools and services built on top of the API and ensured that researchers and archiving institutions could download content and analyse it at scale. From 9 February 2023 this option was removed, to be replaced by a paid-for model out of the reach of all but the most well-financed research institutions. A report in the *Guardian* newspaper published two days before the switch-off noted that it was 'yet another example of the perils of semi-public platforms being controlled by individuals. And an example of the impact that removing or revoking access to a relatively unrecognised backbone of the internet can have on everyday users' (Stokel-Walker 2023).

Restricting access

There are numerous reasons why some cultural heritage collections should not be made openly accessible: open access might harm the communities represented in the collections or negatively impact their interests (for example, social media data collections documenting social protest under authoritarian regimes or activist groups); it might be ethically and/or culturally inappropriate to have certain assets openly accessible to all (for example, for some community and Indigenous archives); there might be ethical limitations arising from concerns around sensitive information, personal data, privacy and confidentiality; or contractual obligations to donors or creators might impose conditions (for example, commercial restrictions or embargoes). Sometimes effective closure of digital collections is the appropriate and ethical path to take, but in other cases cultural heritage institutions can explore ways to make the works they hold more accessible by considering options such as providing clear warnings or contextual explanations, implementing access restrictions, or anonymising or pseudonymising certain types of personal data. In all such instances, the agreement of those with rights or interests in such collections should be sought.

An important example of collection objects for which open access should be questioned is provided by digital surrogates of human remains in GLAM online collections and repositories. Kahn and Simon, in their recent study on this subject, revealed that there are 'no direct limits to access' to various types of digital surrogates of human remains in the collections of digital cultural heritage institutions, besides a couple of warning messages such as a 'statement of intent regarding culturally sensitive items' in the case of the Wellcome Collection in London (Kahn and Simon 2023, 213). However, as they rightly note, 'just because something can be shared, does not automatically mean that it should be' (Kahn and Simon 2023, 222) and critical and responsible digitisation, ingestion and publication practices need to be in place for similar cases. Blanket policies are often unsuitable for dealing with unique objects with a highly specific context, which are better considered on a case-by-case basis.

Infrastructuring access

Sometimes, a first step to openness involves not necessarily providing access to the collections themselves but making available metadata and other forms of derived information. An important recent initiative in the UK, which has the potential to transform access to, if not always (re)use of digital cultural heritage is the Museum Data Service (MDS).[8] Formally launched in 2024, the MDS is a collaboration between Art UK, the Collections Trust and the University of Leicester, with support from Bloomberg Philanthropies and the Arts and Humanities Research Council (AHRC). Like many initiatives before it, it is seeking to solve the challenge of offering search and discovery options across a range of different institutions, with differing approaches to metadata and cataloguing. Projects like Europeana have attempted to do this by developing a network of aggregators, for example Archives Portal Europe, the European Film Gateway and the Digital Repository of Ireland, whose content can be searched through a common interface. The Digital Public Library of America adopted a similar approach, and there are other national and regional examples. The MDS is different in a number of ways: it creates collection level summaries that can be used to gain an overview of the national position; it focuses specifically on data, which it aims to make FAIR; and it is concerned only with museums rather than seeking to range across the GLAM sector. Its ambition is to provide 'the digital standpipe to let decades' worth of knowledge flow and grow' (Museum Data Service n.d.). This kind of approach has also been adopted by curators and archivists working with collections where access is relatively limited because of legislative restriction rather than because of the nature of the content. Material collected under legal deposit legislation, for example, is limited in many countries to access on-site in library reading rooms rather than online. Absent the ability to consult the full UK Web Archive online, the next best thing is access to derived data, including seed lists of the websites crawled for special collections, format profiles (for example, .html, .pdf etc.) and links between archived pages.[9]

In November 2024, the UK's Department for Science, Innovation and Technology confirmed that it is working on the development of a National Data Library of public sector data which sets an ambitious goal to create a new landscape for digital research and cultural heritage.[10] The aim is to bring together existing research programmes that help deliver centralised, secure, data-driven public services to collate and provide access to high-quality data for researchers to explore. There are already existing UK initiatives that have transformed public sector datasets into valuable research assets, such as Administrative Data Research UK, the Integrated Data Service and Health Data Research UK.[11] These services provide a model for offering safe and secure access to data – albeit mostly to accredited specialist researchers rather than to everyone – and present a strong foundation on which to build a potential National Data Library for the benefit of all.

As part of the preparatory work for the development of a UK National Data Library that would make public sector datasets more accessible to researchers and enable future science to thrive, in December 2024 the Wellcome Trust and the Economic and Social Research Council (ESRC) opened a call for the submission of ideas in relation to technical visions and architectures.[12] In January 2025, the UK Government published its AI Opportunities Action Plan, which establishes digital and cultural heritage as a space of technological innovation and discusses in more detail the development of a proposed UK National Data Library. In the Action Plan, cultural heritage organisations are also referred to as bodies holding valuable cultural datasets that could prove to be important for the unlocking of public data assets to enable innovation, research and the generation of value:

> Establish a copyright-cleared British media asset training data set, which can be licensed internationally at scale. This could be done through partnering with bodies that hold valuable cultural data like the National Archives, Natural History Museum, British Library and the BBC to develop a commercial proposition for sharing their data to advance AI.[13]

Access during crisis

We could not finish this chapter without acknowledging the impact of the COVID-19 pandemic on access to GLAM collections, both digital and analogue. From March 2020, cultural heritage institutions around the world began to close their doors to both the public and the majority of their staff. To differing extents, depending on regional and national lockdown arrangements, GLAM collections were physically inaccessible for periods of months over the following two years. Digital access to collections became increasingly important, whether through visiting GLAM websites and image databases, attending webinars and online talks or engaging with increasingly innovative institutional and personal social media channels. Much has already been written about this extraordinary period. Ginzarly and Srour acknowledge that 'As daily-life practices moved online, the COVID-19 crisis was a catalyst for sharing heritage content online'. Focusing on the sharing of content online by means of hashtags allowed for the conceptualisation of 'digitally mediated heritage practices . . . as a process of heritage value co-creation' (Ginzarly and Srour 2022, 3). Burke and colleagues highlight some of the most striking examples of the vibrant co-creative practices that emerged in the museum sector, including, for example, the Getty Museum Challenge, which encouraged social media users to recreate paintings from Getty collections in their own homes, and the launch of #MuseumsUnlocked (Burke, Jørgensen and Jørgensen 2020).

Research is now beginning to engage with the medium-term impact of the necessarily ad-hoc digital innovation that characterised so much of the activity in the cultural sector during the period when audiences were excluded from traditional modes of physical engagement with collections. Samaroudi and colleagues, for example, note that

> through the COVID-19 pandemic the sector has identified audiences and needs with which memory institutions want to engage through digital resources and mechanisms: these include anti-racism activists, audiences characterised through their social condition (lonely, bored) rather than their identity or interests, and those for whom digital may not be an easy or obvious means of communication. (Samaroudi, Echavarria and Perry 2020, 21–22)

It remains to be seen whether insights of this kind will fundamentally alter sector approaches to working with digital cultural heritage, notably in terms of providing access to those who have long been excluded from traditional physical spaces, whether because of disability, location, income or other factors. In terms of what constitutes cultural heritage, Zuanni argues that 'digital content about an object becomes part of this same object's biography, in a complex balance of relationships between original and reproduction, documentation and engagement, reference to the physical counterpart and newborn-digital object' (Zuanni 2023, 696). Here the digital and the analogue are entwined as new forms of cultural heritage emerge and interact.

Notes

1 Transkribus, https://www.transkribus.org/ [accessed 30 January 2025].

2 Tag along with Adler, https://www.zooniverse.org/projects/webster-institute/tag-along-with-adler [accessed 30 January 2025].

3 Congruence Engine was one of five Discovery projects funded by the Arts and Humanities Research Council as part of the Towards a National Collection programme, https://www.sciencemuseumgroup.org.uk/projects/the-congruence-engine [accessed 30 January 2025].

4 OpenGLAM, https://openglam.pubpub.org/ [accessed 30 January 2025].

5 The Principles of Open Scholarly Infrastructure, https://openscholarly infrastructure.org/ [accessed 15 January 2025].

6 Ancestry, https://www.ancestry.co.uk/ [accessed 30 August 2024]; FindMyPast, https://www.findmypast.co.uk/ [accessed 24 November 2025].

7 Wayback Machine, https://web.archive.org/ [accessed 4 September 2024].

8 Museum Data Service, https://museumdata.uk/ [accessed 1 August 2025].

9 Data derived from the UK Web Archive is available via the Shared Research Repository, https://bl.iro.bl.uk/collections/d09fbc16-7a76-49db-a45f-16a99 c30ae3e?locale=en [accessed 17 December 2024].

10 UKAuthority, https://www.ukauthority.com/articles/dsit-confirms-work-on -national-data-library [accessed 5 November 2024].

11 Administrative Data Research UK, https://www.adruk.org/; Integrated Data Service, https://integrateddataservice.gov.uk/; Health Data Research UK, https://www.hdruk.ac.uk/ [accessed 1 August 2025].

12 Wellcome, https://wellcome.org/what-we-do/our-work/uk-data-library [accessed 2 January 2025].

13 Department for Science, Innovation and Technology, 'AI Opportunities Action Plan: Unlocking Data Assets in the Public and Private Sector', https://www.gov.uk/government/publications/ai-opportunities-action-plan/ai -opportunities-action-plan [accessed 21 January 2025].

Chapter 3

Use and reuse

Copyright and licensing

The Berlin Declaration on Open Access (2003) tightly linked ideas of openness to the reality of use and reuse. In order to be considered truly open access, the authors and/or owners of any form of scholarly or cultural output should 'grant to all users a free, irrevocable, worldwide, right of access to, and a license to copy, use, distribute, transmit and display the work publicly and to make and distribute derivative works, in any digital medium for any responsible purpose, subject to proper attribution of authorship' (Max-Planck-Gesellschaft 2003). This leaves no room for doubt that open access involves the purposeful ceding of control over cultural heritage data to unknown publics. Fiona Cameron argues further that restrictions on use do not just affect what happens to cultural heritage today, but in the future: 'copyright, the desire to own and protect data by heritage institutions, acts as an anti-preservationist strategy' (Cameron 2021, 46).

But questions of copyright, use and reuse remain highly contested. Copyright is one of the most common forms of intellectual property rights present in digital cultural heritage. The terms of copyright differ slightly between countries, but it always has a common aim: to enable creators to benefit from and control the distribution of their work by preventing its unauthorised reuse. Copyright complexities, and issues that arise from the provision of access to and use of digital cultural heritage assets, require a combination of expertise – from cultural heritage professionals, legislators, lawyers and copyright experts – to unpack them. A range of practice exists within the cultural heritage sector, some arising from policy decisions within collecting/archiving institutions and some the result of external legal frameworks. In the UK, for example, the UK Libraries and Archives Copyright Alliance (LACA) is the main UK body lobbying on behalf of library, information and archive professionals, and users of GLAM institutions, for fair practices in copyright. It advocates for a fair and balanced copyright framework that represents the rights of copyright holders while placing equal value on the importance of users' liberties. In 2014, the Association of European Research Libraries (LIBER) set up a working group on Copyright and Legal questions, which consists of librarians, lawyers, academics and communications professionals who monitor current European law and react to proposed changes on behalf of libraries, archives, researchers and students. The working group offers support to cultural heritage professionals engaged in research who seek to acquire the training to understand the complex landscape of copyright for cultural heritage assets. Since 2010 the International Council of Archives (ICA) has been represented at the World Intellectual Property Organization's (WIPO) Standing Committee on Copyright and Related Rights (SCCR), which focuses on copyright advocacy work to support the archival mission. Working together with the International Federation of Library Associations and Institutions (IFLA) and the International Council of Museums (ICOM), the SCCR's goal is 'a binding international treaty setting out basic copyright exceptions that would enable libraries, archives, and museums around the globe to fulfil their mission to preserve their holdings and make them available for use' (Dryden 2024).

Copyright, however, is not the only factor in determining the permitted uses and reuse of cultural heritage materials. In the UK and many other countries, the exploitation of some forms of born-digital material is restricted by the terms of legal deposit legislation. It is not, for example, possible to cut and paste text from an archived web page held in the UK Web Archive at the British Library, or indeed to take a screenshot or use any other form of image capture (Milligan 2015). In other cases, restrictions arise from the economic imperatives at work within the cultural heritage sector. Some institutions choose to impose restrictions on the use and reuse of collection images so that income can be generated from their sale, either via a third-party image library or an in-house platform. However, as Patricia Huang notes, while 'At the beginning of [the] information revolution, museums were understood to have high hopes for the revenue that digital image licensing (DIL) services might generate . . . DIL services in museums have yet to report significant profits'. Consequently, 'a growing number of art history museums have chosen to encourage free or CC-licensed distribution of their images' (Huang 2020, 220).

The 'CC' referenced by Huang is Creative Commons, an international non-profit organisation that seeks to empower 'individuals and communities around the world by equipping them with technical, legal, and policy solutions to enable sharing of knowledge and culture in the public interest' (Creative Commons n.d.-c). Creative Commons, and specifically the suite of licences that it has produced to enable different forms of sharing and reuse, has become an essential part of the scholarly and cultural heritage open-data landscape. At the time of writing, there are six CC licences available, ranging from CC BY, which simply requires an acknowledgement of authorship, to CC BY-NC-ND, which allows attributed sharing but prevents commercial use and the creation of any form of derivative work. Most permissive of all, and reflecting the requirements of the Berlin Declaration, is the CC0 public domain dedication tool, which allows authors, creators and owners to waive any interests in their works so that they can be freely reused and remixed (Creative Commons n.d.-b). The Walters Art Museum in Baltimore, Maryland, was an early institution to adopt CC licensing for its collection images, removing copyright restrictions from more than 10,000 images in 2011 (Walters Art Museum 2011).[1] Other, larger institutions followed, for example the Rijksmuseum in Amsterdam allows the 'use of digital reproductions of public domain objects made available . . . without permission being required. For commercial purposes too' (Rijksmuseum n.d.). Creative Commons itself developed a 'search portal' that allows users to explore content that 'you can share, use, and remix' (Creative Commons n.d.-a). Numerous online image searches, for example those offered by Google Images and Wikimedia Commons, offer an option to filter according to copyright and/or licensing status so that users can be reasonably confident they are allowed to use the digital images they find for research and creative practice.

Any barrier placed in the way of reuse, for example the insistence on those elements of a Creative Commons licence that prohibit the creation of derivative works or commercial use, constrains how users can interact with digital cultural heritage beyond simply looking at or reading it. Such restrictions would prohibit innovation of the kind evident from the collaboration between the British Library and the British Fashion Council, which recognises the work of student fashion designers who draw inspiration from the Library's online collections. In 2021, for example, the Public Award was given to Chiara Lamon, whose designs used images from the British Library's collections that 'included the work of photographer Ethienne Jules, images from geology and dance and a comparison of a multiple collar garment from Viktor and Rolf's Autumn/Winter 2003 collection paired with an early portrait of a man in a collared shirt' (British Library n.d.). This kind of imaginative repurposing and remixing of digital cultural heritage cannot easily be anticipated, but it can be closed off by the use of restrictive licensing.

Licences, and in particular open licences, 'are the key mechanism for ensuring that works can be used and reused legally' (Hamilton and Saunderson 2017, 3). Licensing and the open movement partly developed as a reaction to the presence of intellectual property rights. Open licences, such as the Creative Commons licences, and open source licences, for example MIT GPLv3 and others, are tools that were created to remove legal barriers, making it easier to share copyrighted content and communicate reuse conditions in a simple way, thereby encouraging the maximum public reuse of cultural heritage data. Beyond licensing, the reuse of copyrighted GLAM content is further enabled in the UK by the Copyright, Designs and Patents Act 1988,[2] in the EU via the Directive on Copyright in the Digital Market (hereafter EU Directive)[3] through the introduction of text and data mining exceptions for the purpose of scientific research, and in the USA through the 'fair use' doctrine.

Navigating grey areas of reuse

Although licences succeed in preventing copyrighted digital cultural heritage from being locked down, there remains copyrighted content that cannot be treated within this framework, resulting in what has become known in the digital cultural heritage community as the 'twentieth-century black hole'. This neat phrase refers to the very low quantity of twentieth-century material that is available for reuse because of the difficulty in clearing – or even determining – rights (Boyle 2009). Both out-of-commerce works (OOCWs) – that is, works that are either protected by copyright but not available commercially or have never been and/or were never intended to be available commercially (for example unpublished works, grey literature, amateur photography and certain expressions of traditional culture) – and orphan works, for which the rightsholder is not known or cannot be found (Martinez and Terras 2019), are still causing headaches for cultural heritage professionals in terms of their reuse status. There have been several recent legislative attempts to systematically address these issues, especially through the adoption of the EU Directive noted previously, which introduces a legal framework to support cultural heritage institutions in the digitisation and cross-border dissemination of OOCWs. This was followed by the launch in 2021 of the European Union Intellectual Property Office (EUIPO) Out-Of-Commerce Works Portal, where heritage institutions and other organisations can share information about out-of-commerce works to ensure that they are accessible to the public;[4] and the EUIPO Orphan Works Database, which provides information about orphan works contained in the collections of publicly accessible cultural heritage institutions.[5]

Not surprisingly, for born-digital cultural heritage there are significant uncertainties and grey areas in relation to intellectual property rights, permissions, privacy and licences that further hinder its use and reuse. While she is primarily concerned with the relationship between copyright and the preservation of born-digital materials, the issues identified by Katherine Fisher similarly affect end users: researchers and practitioners are faced with 'shifting definitions of ownership, unclear distinctions between published and unpublished content, digital rights management laws and technologies, and the layered copyrights that can exist in complex digital objects and their dependencies' (Fisher 2021, 238).

Copyright brings challenges for the reuse of digital cultural heritage content even by its absence. Although in theory, once copyright protection expires, a creative work automatically falls into the public domain and anyone can reuse it for any purpose without obtaining permission, cultural heritage institutions still engage in the practice of claiming copyright over faithful digitised and born-digital surrogates of public domain works (Wallace and Euler 2020; Wallace 2022a). Even if a number of legislative interventions have been introduced aiming to ensure that public domain works remain in the public domain once digitised, for example Article 14 of the EU Directive, which aims to prohibit public domain 'works of visual art' from being subjected to new copyright claims, 'we are still talking about copyright because the overwhelming majority of cultural institutions assert copyright in surrogates despite its unsound legal basis' (Wallace 2022b, 329).

Reusing cultural heritage collections as data

Navigating rights, restrictions and other legal obstacles is just one piece of the complex matrix that impacts wider reuse of digital and born-digital cultural heritage collections and the ability to scale up innovative research and creative work around them. Licensing and the OpenGLAM movement, along with the wealth of digitised and born-digital cultural heritage collections that have resulted from the large-scale digitisation efforts of the last decades, have allowed researchers and cultural heritage professionals to conceptualise 'cultural heritage data as humanities research data' (Tasovac, Chambers and Tóth-Czifra 2020, 1), as well as to start thinking and working 'at scale' with digital cultural heritage data. As Daniel Wilson argues, '"scale" has become a zeitgeist, in particular for the digital humanities, increasingly coupled to the field of data science, its methods, thought-style and knowledge claims' (Wilson 2022). It is often in GLAM labs within cultural heritage organisations that we have witnessed this interdisciplinary and experimental work flourishing over the last years: researchers, cultural heritage professionals and data scientists collaboratively working towards the development and reuse of extensive collections of in-copyright and/or licensed cultural heritage materials to carry out various types of data-driven humanities research (for example, text mining, data mining, data visualisation, mapping, image analysis, audio analysis, network analysis, machine learning) (Candela et al. 2020).

In order to address this recent computational turn in cultural heritage, since 2016 the Collections-as-Data movement, and particularly the Always Already Computational project (Padilla et al. 2019) and its Mellon-funded successor, Collections as Data: Part to Whole (Padilla et al. 2023), has been focusing on and advocating for the responsible development and computational use of digitised and born-digital cultural heritage collections by making these collections available as data that is 'amenable to computation' (Padilla et al. 2019, 20). The Collections-as-Data movement and community of practice have blossomed internationally and have been advocating for the importance of presenting cultural heritage collections in open, reusable formats as machine-readable data, through the Santa Barbara Statement on Collections as Data (2019) and the Vancouver Statement on Collections as Data (2023).[6] Furthermore, Collections-as-Data is focused on promoting and encouraging diverse forms of collaboration among stakeholders and areas of work that need to be brought together to responsibly develop and support the reuse of collections as data, including reference services, documentation, repository development, collections management, digitisation, web archiving, outreach and preservation. The movement also highlights concerns about ethical stewardship, social and technical interoperability, transparent documentation, commitments to preservation and responsible operations (Padilla 2019; Padilla et al. 2023).

Aligned with Collections-as-Data's mission to advance the responsible development and computational reuse of digital cultural heritage collections, a series of initiatives have introduced the importance of producing datasheets (Alkemade et al. 2023) and data envelopes (Luthra and Eskevich 2024). Especially in light of developments in AI and the need for high-quality, well-documented GLAM datasets for machine learning processes, these datasheets and data envelopes are designed to provide context for and transparent information about provenance, purposes, composition, collection processes, recommended uses or societal biases reflected in cultural heritage datasets. Developing, providing and maintaining digital cultural heritage collections as data is not an easy task for cultural heritage institutions, and to support adoption in a 'business-as-usual' mode, a number of checklists and guidelines have been developed to help them break down the tasks, steps and requirements for such an endeavour (Candela et al. 2023; Lee 2023).

Technical frameworks

Earlier technical attempts to offer GLAM datasets for reuse include the Open Archives Initiative Protocol for Metadata Harvesting (OAI-PMH), which provided links to zipped collections or to static collection directories that can be accessed via GitHub, such as those of The New York Public Library,[7] The Cooper Hewitt Museum[8] and The Tate Collection.[9] Over the last ten years, the most common way for museums and other GLAMS to openly release their collection data has been via an API. APIs are a way of structuring data that makes it accessible and transmissible in a machine-readable and dynamic way, allowing for communication between software programs. From the perspective of a cultural heritage institution, an API allows users to request data from inside the institution and have it delivered to them in a usable form, freely available by means of an open licence which is Creative Commons (CC) or CC-like.

Although API technology has become widely used in the GLAM world in general, a recent audit showed that there is some resistance to or delay in the adoption of APIs among GLAM institutions, particularly in the UK. Almost half (49 per cent) of respondents to a 2022 survey said that their institution did not have APIs; only 21 per cent said that their institution had an API that allows others to make use of their online collections; and a further 16 per cent said that the introduction of an API was pending (Gosling et al. 2022, 3). Moreover, the existing open APIs have low levels of usage and some either struggle to perform or stall completely when attempting higher-volume queries for collaborative research projects (Gosling et al. 2022, 5). Indeed, there is very little research aiming to understand how people use collections data from cultural heritage institutions through APIs (Villaespesa et al. 2021), thus limiting our capacity to assess the quality of and interest in reusing the available data and to encourage straightforward engagement with APIs by users with a range of technical expertise. For example, the Museums of the City of Paris/Paris Musées make available more than 100,000 open-access works via their GraphQL API, but an additional layer of authentication is required for the user to acquire the API's key and access its content (in JSON files).[10] This adds friction to the process and discourages serendipitous rather than targeted exploration. Similarly, the technical documentation and development for both the V&A Collections API[11] and the Wellcome Collection API[12] are designed for and addressed to developers as end-users, as per their domain names. This is suggestive of a high barrier to entry and likely to discourage general research use.

Intended for users who might benefit from practical, accessible examples, rather than exhaustive technical specifications, the Jupyter Notebook is becoming a key tool for GLAM institutions to introduce users to accessing and reusing their datasets (Candela et al. 2023). The Jupyter Notebook is a web application, often used as a learning and teaching environment, which allows users to craft easily shared, interactive, computational narratives that mix live code, results and text. The value of Jupyter Notebooks for GLAM services and collections data has been demonstrated in recent years by the GLAM Workbench (Sherratt 2021), focusing mainly on the GLAM sector in Australia and New Zealand, but also encompassing material from the UK Web and UK Government Web Archives. These 'workbenches' succeed not only in making GLAM data more accessible by using Jupyter Notebooks to analyse and reuse it, but also establish these processes as highly reproducible, even by users without coding skills. The National Library of Scotland's Digital Scholarship Service has been using Jupyter Notebooks to support its release of collections as data (including digitised collections (text and images); metadata collections; map data; and organisational data) via its data-delivery platform, the Data Foundry, since September 2019.[13] Based on the principles of openness, transparency, reproducibility and practicality, the Data Foundry is designed to be easy to access and use, providing 'no-nonsense' data with clear rights information, straightforward downloads, dataset trials and plain-text-only options. The Jupyter Notebooks were created initially as 'a COVID-19 response' in order 'to give all library users an opportunity to explore the Library's collections as data, even if they have never programmed or conducted data analysis' (Ames and Havens 2022, 52).

Documentation and standards

Reuse can take many forms and the concept itself is multifaceted. The editorial note that accompanies a special issue of the *International Journal on Digital Libraries* on 'FAIR data and cultural heritage' focuses on the final letter of the acronym, suggesting that 'to reuse data in cultural heritage it is necessary to expand the "R" facet of the FAIR principles at least into R3: Reusable, Relevant and Reliable' (Hermon and Niccolucci 2021, 251). However, preparing digital cultural heritage data to be reused is a resource-intensive process for cultural heritage institutions and stakeholders, requiring time, expertise and robust infrastructure. The quest for data interoperability has been one of the major challenges in digital cultural heritage since its early days and a vast array of standards and technical solutions have been explored and developed over the years to support and encourage cultural heritage data interchange and reuse among different audiences (Ioannides, Georgopoulos and Scherer 2005).

Digital cultural heritage standards are like a 'shared grammar', establishing a common way of structuring, understanding and managing information, and they can take all sorts of forms and shapes and be applied to a wide variety of assets or concepts. Among the most popular and widely used standards in the digital cultural heritage sector is the CIDOC Conceptual Reference Model (CRM), a knowledge representation model 'for describing the implicit and explicit concepts and relationships used in cultural heritage documentation' (CIDOC CRM n.d.). CIDOC CRM provides a common and extensible semantic framework for evidence-based cultural heritage information integration and reuse. Persistent identifiers (PIDs), on the other hand, are globally unique and long-lasting references to potentially any sort of digital entity and their adoption through the form of Archival Resource Keys (ARKs)[14] or Digital Object Identifiers (DOIs)[15] sits at the foundation of the FAIR principles by making cultural heritage data interoperable and encouraging reuse. Being able to uniquely identify digital or born-digital cultural heritage objects supports their discovery, curation and reuse – you cannot provide persistent or even consistent access to an item in order to reuse it if you do not know what it is. The importance of persistent identifiers is best realised through considering what happens when digital cultural heritage collections do not have a PID strategy: broken links, link rot and dying data, which affects not only the user experience but also all forms of data (re)use.

In the area of collections management, metadata standards, such as the Metadata Encoding and Transmission Standard (METS) created by the Library of Congress in the US, or Spectrum, the UK museum collections management standard that is also used around the world, are designed to describe and structure digital cultural heritage content in standardised human- and machine-readable ways and further enable its interchange and reuse. Finally, the International Image Interoperability Framework (IIIF) is a set of standards for interoperable functionality in digital image repositories, allowing users to choose different viewers and tools to interact with cultural heritage content.[16] IIIF leverages interoperability and the fabric of the web to access new possibilities for image-based resources, while reducing long-term maintenance and technological lock-in.

Standards are capable of breaking data out of 'silos' and enabling the interchange and reuse of digital cultural heritage data, but Linked Data and semantic web technologies are able to truly reap the benefits of the reuse and interconnection of digital cultural heritage at scale. Originating from the concept of the World Wide Web, the semantic web has as its main purpose the interconnection of data through a set of tools and techniques to structure and relate information on the web so that it can be shared, discovered, integrated and reused efficiently by both humans and machines. Cultural heritage data is highly heterogeneous, multilingual, semantically rich and distributed, and in order to achieve interoperable creation, publication and reuse of such rich and varied content, information must be available in a standardised, searchable format through the application of the principles and technologies of Linked Open Data (LOD) and semantic web technologies (Jones and Seikel 2016; Bikakis et al. 2021).

Embracing a Linked Open cultural heritage data approach makes it possible to connect data from different institutions to enable better inter-operability between collections and better opportunities for researchers and developers to use that data. A popular approach is to use Wikidata, a form of community-curated LOD, as a node for linking different cultural heritage datasets. Llyfrgell Genedlaethol Cymru/the National Library of Wales has been pioneering in using Wikidata to explore the benefits of LOD, from improving access to collections to data and metadata enrichment. In early 2016 a Wikipedian in residence, Jason Evans, and a Wikidata visiting scholar, Simon Cobb, converted a mass of library collections into Wikidata – free, open, linked data that anyone can access, interpret and visualise (Evans and Cobb 2016). Using Wikidata to connect common data elements such as people and places has helped to create rich bilingual data which can be freely reused with an internet connection and access to a computer or other digital device. This example highlights the benefit of adopting open common data standards to streamline services, improve discoverability within datasets and open up opportunities for new collaborations and the creative reuses that can come from sharing such rich data without restrictions. Following this attempt, the Semantic Name Authority Repository Cymru (SNARC)[17] was established by the Wikipedian in order to provide

> a central hub for name authority records relating to Wales and in the Welsh language . . . Based on Wikidata, but using a simplified and customised ontology, the data is presented as Linked Open Data and this makes it easier for us to define relationships between entities in our collections. All the data is bilingual and available on an Open Licence . . . Our goal is to grow the dataset using data from Welsh cultural organisations, connecting our heritage in one central hub. It will also act as an important bridge between 3rd party linked open data from Wikidata and other sources, and data curated by GLAM professionals around the world. (SNARC n.d.)

Using Wikidata shows that it is perfectly possible to work with linked open cultural heritage data without developing costly, proprietary, independent platforms that require advanced expertise in knowledge representation and semantic technologies, as well as resources for ongoing management, storage, hosting and continuous development. On the other hand, semantic web technologies also lie at the heart of many large-scale infrastructural investments in the area of cultural heritage, such as the Europeana aggregator and the newly established European Collaborative Cloud for Cultural Heritage (ECCCH), developed by ECHOES (European Cloud for Heritage OpEn Science).[18] The latter project, funded by the European Commission and UK Research and Innovation (UKRI), brings together fragmented communities in the cultural heritage field into a new community around the digital commons. It remains to be seen where the idea for a UK National Data Library, discussed earlier, falls between these two poles.

Skills and training

To fully harness the potential of the recent computational turn in cultural heritage, a range of training initiatives and open educational resources have been developed to build capacity among professionals working within and alongside the cultural heritage sector as well as to support researchers in reusing digital cultural heritage datasets and collections. For example, The Programming Historian recently collaborated with The National Archives, UK and Jisc to produce a special series of open educational resources focused on computational analysis of large-scale digital cultural heritage collections.[19] Similarly, Library Carpentry develops and delivers workshops to equip librarians and other information professionals in the GLAM sector with essential computational skills.[20] Other notable training opportunities include initiatives like the Europeana Academy,[21] the Cambridge Cultural Heritage Data School,[22] the DARIAH-Campus courses focused on digital cultural heritage[23] and Towards Digital Collections: Resources for Galleries, Libraries, Archives and Museums,[24] produced as part of the Towards a National Collection programme.

The increasing demand for advanced data literacy within the cultural heritage sector, and the consequent training requirements, have gradually led to the establishment of digital cultural heritage as a recognised academic discipline at university level. For instance, since 2018 the University of Edinburgh has hosted a chair in digital cultural heritage, supported by initiatives like the Digital Cultural Heritage Research Network (DCHRN) and a dedicated Digital Cultural Heritage cluster,[25] with a recent MSc in Cultural Heritage Futures.[26] Similarly, the University of Glasgow has embraced this field with its Arts and Humanities Partnership Catalyst for Digital Cultural

Heritage.[27] Additional programmes, such as the MSc in Digital Heritage at the University of York,[28] further demonstrate the integration of digital perspectives into the academic study of cultural heritage.

Restricting reuse

There are often, however, good reasons for restricting the uses to which digital cultural heritage can be put, and for the nuanced application of licensing to whole or partial collections. A recent challenge to forward-looking cultural heritage organisations that have previously allowed various kinds of use and reuse of their data has been posed by the Large Language Models (LLMs) that underpin Generative AI. LLMs and the companies behind them are hungry for data to train their models, and cultural heritage organisations, like many other bodies and organisations that post content online, are sources of high-quality data. Many LLMs have been trained on openly available cultural heritage datasets or creative works from various knowledge sectors, often without permission or credit. However, the ongoing legal uncertainty surrounding AI model training has made institutions increasingly hesitant or unwilling to share their content, reversing progress made over the past two decades towards greater openness and accessibility of their data. While the regulation of copyright and licensing for AI training data and outputs is still evolving – various countries are exploring approaches such as text and data mining exceptions, transparency measures and technical standards – GLAM institutions and stakeholders are responding in various ways to address the ongoing legal grey area, ranging from limiting access to their collections to implementing innovative strategies for monitoring and preventing unauthorised use of their datasets.

The National Library of the Netherlands, for example, has restricted access to its online collections for 'commercial parties who crawl digital resources on websites on a large scale for training models', using a combination of 'technical measures' and changes to terms of use. It remains committed to encouraging 'academic research based on our collections as much as possible. We guarantee that this reuse shall not be hindered by our measures against AI companies' (National Library of the Netherlands n.d.). This is a difficult balance to strike for GLAMs that, for over a decade now, have been focusing on developing a strong culture of openness in relation to their digital collections. The potential ethical and legal problems posed by the use of Generative AI in this space (for example, copyright, data protection and ethical sensitivities) are still very much emerging and add a new layer of complexity to the discussion about openness and the use and reuse of digital cultural heritage collections. A more drastic solution to prevent the unauthorised exploitation of artistic works is offered by tools such as Nightshade, developed at the University of Chicago. Nightshade is 'a tool that turns any image into a data sample that is unsuitable for model training. More precisely, Nightshade transforms images into "poison" samples, so that models training on them without consent will see their models learn unpredictable behaviors that deviate from expected norms' (The Nightshade Team n.d.). This is a highly contested and rapidly changing area of research and practice, and there is potential for erosion of public trust not just in AI but in the institutions who may wish to share their data and collaborate with technology companies.

The growing focus on use and reuse in relation to digital cultural heritage – by cultural heritage institutions themselves, by researchers and practitioners, by a range of other users and stakeholders – speaks to the enormous potential value of this new form of heritage material and indicates a growing willingness to embrace openness, transparency and even a relative loss of control over some forms of collections data. Standards, documentation, new tools and technologies, and training and skills are part of the solution to encouraging new and innovative uses of digital cultural heritage, but they also hint at some of the challenges to be faced. Capacity building and effective resourcing are essential if progress is to be sustained and further imaginative reuse encouraged and supported where appropriate.

Notes

1 The licence chosen was the very first iteration of the CC0 Universal Deed, https://creativecommons.org/publicdomain/zero/1.0/deed.en [accessed 4 September 2024].

2 Copyright, Designs and Patents Act 1988, https://www.legislation.gov.uk/ukpga/1988/48/section/29A [accessed 30 January 2025].

3 Directive on Copyright in the Digital Market, https://eur-lex.europa.eu/eli/dir/2019/790/oj [accessed 30 January 2025].

4 EUIPO Out-Of-Commerce Works Portal, https://euipo.europa.eu/out-of-commerce/ [accessed 30 January 2025].

5 EUIPO Orphan Works Database, https://euipo.europa.eu/orphanworks/ [accessed 30 January 2025].

6 The Santa Barbara Statement on Collections as Data, https://collectionsasdata.github.io/statement/; the Vancouver Statement on Collections as Data, https://zenodo.org/records/8342171 [accessed 20 January 2025].

7 New York Public Library, https://github.com/NYPL-publicdomain/data-and-utilities [accessed 30 January 2025].

8 The Cooper Hewitt Museum, https://github.com/cooperhewitt/collection [accessed 30 January 2025].

9 The Tate Collection, https://github.com/tategallery/collection [accessed 30 January 2025].

10 Museums of the City of Paris/Paris Musées, https://apicollections.parismusees.paris.fr/ [accessed 30 January 2025].

11 V&A Collections, https://developers.vam.ac.uk/ [accessed 30 January 2025].

12 Wellcome Collection, https://developers.wellcomecollection.org/ [accessed 30 January 2025].

13 Data Foundry, National Library of Scotland, https://data.nls.uk/ [accessed 30 January 2025].

14 Archival Resource Keys, https://arks.org/ [accessed 30 January 2025].

15 Digital Object Identifiers, https://www.doi.org/ [accessed 30 January 2025].

16 International Image Interoperability Framework, https://iiif.io/ [accessed 30 January 2025].

17 Semantic Name Authority Repository Cymru, https://snarc-llgc.wikibase.cloud/wiki/Main_Page [accessed 30 January 2025].

18 European Collaborative Cloud for Cultural Heritage, https://www.echoes-eccch.eu/ [accessed 30 January 2025].

19 The Programming Historian, https://programminghistorian.org/en/jisc-tna-partnership [accessed 30 January 2025].

20 Library Carpentry, https://librarycarpentry.org/ [accessed 30 January 2025].

21 Europeana Academy, https://pro.europeana.eu/page/europeana-academy [accessed 30 January 2025].

22 Cambridge Cultural Heritage Data School, https://www.cdh.cam.ac.uk/events/39077/ [accessed 30 January 2025].

23 DARIAH-Campus, https://www.dariah.eu/2024/11/01/dariah-campus-courses-on-digital-cultural-heritage-a-path-through-cultural-heritage-data-data-modelling-and-europeana-apis/ [accessed 30 January 2025].

24 Towards Digital Collections, https://www.towardsdigitalcollections.org/ [accessed 30 January 2025].

25 Digital Cultural Heritage Research Network, https://dchrn.de.ed.ac.uk/ [accessed 30 January 2025].

26 Cultural Heritage Futures, https://efi.ed.ac.uk/programmes/cultural -heritage-futures [accessed 30 January 2025].

27 University of Glasgow College of Arts and Humanities, https://www.gla.ac.uk /colleges/arts/knowledge-exchange/catalyst/ [accessed 30 January 2025].

28 Digital Heritage (MSc), https://www.york.ac.uk/study/postgraduate-taught /courses/msc-digital-heritage/ [accessed 30 January 2025].

Chapter 4

Value(s)

Measuring impact and value

As neatly summarised by Azzopardi and colleagues, 'Value is a foundational idea in the heritage sector, where heritage values are understood in two different ways: the value *of* heritage objects and the values held *for* heritage objects. In both, heritage values are contextual values' (Azzopardi et al. 2023, 371). Notions of value can be extremely broad – 'For UNESCO anything considered important enough to be passed on to the future can be considered to have heritage value of some kind' (Cameron 2021, 61) – or highly constrained, for example by the remit of a particular memory institution or the interests of a particular community or group. As Beel and Wallace acknowledge, '"Cultural value" as a concept is both intuitively understandable but at the same time empirically difficult to tie down' (Beel and Wallace 2020, 3). It can be contingent on locality, chronology, form, community and/or a range of other explicit or tacit assumptions and understandings. For Rizzo and Mignosa, 'cultural heritage is a complex and elusive concept, changing constantly through time, combining cultural, aesthetic, symbolic, spiritual, historical and economic values' (Rizzo and Mignosa 2013, xxiv).

This lack of certainty about what constitutes value is perhaps even more marked in relation to digital cultural heritage. This is a new form of cultural output, even though it exists within established narratives about cultural value and the systems that help to ascribe such value(s). One factor that influences how we respond to digital objects and data as cultural heritage is our awareness of risk, not just to highly specialised forms of digital cultural heritage but to any form of digital output. This will be discussed in more detail in Chapter 5, but as Fiona Cameron identifies, 'Digital data is . . . the new cultural heritage of life, one that is increasingly threatened and therefore valued' (Cameron 2021, 3). It is vulnerability rather than scarcity or rarity that is deemed relevant here.

Some digital cultural heritage is, of course, characterised by rarity or uniqueness. Much of the born-digital art and culture preserved by Rhizome, for example, falls into this category.[1] Its NetArt Anthology presents 100 'exemplary works', a term that highlights preservation while also indicating wider cultural loss, from the 1980s to the 2010s. The uniqueness of the artworks is drawn out in descriptions of the complex process of remediation involved in preserving and presenting each of them. Eduardo Kac's *Reabracadabra* (1985) is just one such example:

> The data for the characters that made up 'Reabracadabra' were saved on an 8-inch floppy disk, but Kac lacked access to the proprietary Minitel editing platform necessary to run it. When the videotexto signal went dark in the mid-1990s, the work became entirely inaccessible . . . The work has now been reconstructed by the artist with the assistance of the PAMAL research unit at l'Ecole Supérieure d'Art d'Avignon – using a legacy machine and mimicking dial-up download speeds – but the network it was a part of is no more. (Rhizome n.d.)

Digital cultural heritage, however, is more often marked by scale, and indeed duplication. Web archives, for example, are characterised by high levels of duplication: writing about the Portuguese Web Archive in 2006, Gomes and colleagues noted that 'over 25% of the documents kept in the archive were exact duplicates' (819). Sophisticated deduplication strategies have since been developed, but as Pennock (2013) acknowledges, 'There are cases where de-duplication is not desirable as it conflicts with the preservation intent and business case of the collecting institution' (14). There is no one model of preservation that works in all circumstances and contexts.

There have been numerous attempts to quantify and measure the value of more traditional forms of cultural heritage (see, for example, Klamer 2013; Rizzo and Mignosa 2013; Wright and Eppink 2016), and that work is continuing in the digital sphere. Reflecting on the concept of value, both as a social and economic variable, in the digital cultural heritage sector, Lorna Hughes, in her edited volume *Evaluating and Measuring the Value, Use and Impact of Digital Collections*, suggests that 'Digital collections are valuable to different audiences for different reasons. Value is subjective, changes over time, and has different meanings that are contingent on external factors' (Hughes 2012, 5). Indeed, conceptualising and measuring the value of digital cultural heritage, using both quantitative and qualitative metrics, is an ongoing challenge.

Partly as a means to incentivise the adoption of digital work in cultural heritage institutions and attract corresponding funding, since the mid-2000s there has been a growing focus on assessing and showcasing the value that can accrue from digital cultural heritage in order to demonstrate the return-on-investment from its creation. Early in her book *Digitizing Collections: Strategic Issues for the Information Manager*, Hughes addresses the factors that make digital cultural heritage collections 'valuable' to different communities, focusing on access, supporting preservation, collections development and institutional and strategic benefit. On the other hand, she also highlights the impact of digital collections on institutions' planning, including the need for new business models to support the development and maintenance of digital collections, the institutional costs and benefits of digital collections and the intellectual implications of changes to the way data is used and managed and of new forms of scholarship (Hughes 2004).

In 2012, Simon Tanner developed the 'Balanced Value Impact Model' (BVIM), a systematic way to measure and elucidate the impact of GLAM digital resources and collections more accurately, by revealing at the highest level benefits such as 'learning; research; consumption; strengthening communities; building collaboration and the British university brand' (Tanner 2012, 21). This model and its principles have been widely used across the cultural heritage sector and especially in the development of the Europeana Impact Playbook (2017), which aimed to support cultural heritage organisations and professionals in assessing the impact and value of their digital cultural heritage activities. The Impact Playbook made the important case for assessing the impact of institutions' digital cultural heritage practices by measuring changes in stakeholders and audiences. It foregrounded the concept of the 'ripple effect' to assess these flexible and ongoing processes, which usually take place over a long period of time: 'each change creates the conditions for another change that leads to another change and another, and so on' (Europeana Impact Playbook 2017, Introduction: What is Impact?). A practical way to assess impact is through the implementation of 'value lenses', originally proposed by Tanner in his BVIM to describe the 'types of value that are most commonly connected with the experience of interacting with digital cultural heritage' (Europeana Impact Playbook 2017).[2] The five value lenses approach, comprising the utility lens, the existence lens, the legacy lens, the learning lens and the community lens, was one of the first attempts to systematise and discuss the different kinds of value digital resources can have, but it was not widely adopted in the cultural heritage sector.

More recently, a Europeana report on 'Measuring the instances and value of digital cultural heritage reuse' introduced the concept of 'reuse indicators' to understand and assess instances of the reuse of digital heritage content and the (potential) value that this creates (Vasileva and McNeilly 2024). This report, with its introduction of the concept of 'reuse' as a value indicator, was published after more than a decade of initiatives such as OpenGLAM and the Collections-as-Data movement, and indeed Europeana itself, advocating for and promoting open access, open licensing and the computational reuse of digital cultural heritage data. The Europeana report makes two important comments around reuse indicators. First, while the general impact and reuse indicators tracked by cultural heritage institutions are often 'simple', quantifiable, useful for reporting metrics and focus on, for example, downloads, visits (logs), social media metrics or mentions in academic publications, they alone do not provide sufficiently rich information and bear no relation to the quality of the engagement and accrued value. Capturing reuse cases, both manually and, more recently, through automated (AI) tools, is crucial to gain greater insight into the value generated through the reuse of digital cultural heritage content. An additional way in which to improve processes for capturing the reuse of GLAM data is the documentation of GLAM datasets as research outputs via datasheets (Alkemade et al. 2023) and assigning them PIDs, such as DOIs, so that their reuse can be machine traceable. On the other hand, reuse audiences, the 'who' when considering reuse, and reuse scenarios for these audiences are often not well articulated or studied. The type of reuse – its purpose and context – differs across communities or industries: cultural heritage professionals, educators, researchers, cultural enthusiasts and the wider public, as well as comparatively new or lesser-known target audiences such as the gaming and tourism sectors, the media and the creative industries. As Vasileva and McNeilly argue in their Europeana report, 'quantitative research is used effectively in the analysis of user segmentation that can help to better understand the purposes of data reuse, but not (yet) its value. There are thus opportunities to build more meaningful metrics for reuse in different industries and according to different user profiles' (Vasileva and McNeilly 2024, 16).

Uzelac and Higgins (2025) have surveyed a range of work concerned with assessing the impact of cultural initiatives in the EU, exploring how data can be used to demonstrate impact and hence value. Their conclusion, that 'despite decades of continuous investment in the development of digital cultural resources within an ever-evolving digital landscape, there is still no clear consensus on how to assess the impact of digital heritage resources and projects', emphasises just how challenging work in this field can be. They identify failure to translate theoretical frameworks for impact assessment into practice as one of the key barriers to demonstrating value of many different kinds (12), a common thread in the initiatives mentioned previously. They conclude by highlighting the need for significant further research, which 'should prioritize critical case studies that incorporate qualitative and quantitative data, comparative studies across different types of LAM [Libraries, Archives and Museums] institutions and longitu- dinal studies to identify trends' (13).

Language also matters when assessing the impact and value of digital cultural heritage collections. In her study on the impact of digitised special library collections in the UK, Christina Kamposiori argues that the language deployed in the impact definitions used by funders and institutions (espe- cially university libraries), with its strong focus on research and the Research Excellence Framework (REF) criteria, 'cannot always communicate the value and positive effect of the audience-focused strategies and activities led by libraries' (Kamposiori 2020, 12). Indeed, GLAMs often use terms such as 'engagement' to refer to the impact and value of their digital or born-digital collections for their target and wider audiences and there is a strong and diverse body of research around capturing and enhancing user engagement with digital and born-digital cultural heritage collections (Bailey-Ross et al. 2017; Agosti, Orio and Ponchia 2018; Speakman, Hall and Walsh 2018).

While the reuse, impact and value of GLAM collections in advancing research and scholarship have been actively advocated for and assessed over the last decade, it is only very recently that the community has started to explore the commercial and non-commercial reuse of openly licensed digital cultural heritage data as a source of economic value (Valeonti, Terras and Hudson-Smith 2020). Moreover, a recent study from The Creative Informatics Programme at the University of Edinburgh showcased how mass-digitised cultural heritage content, underpinned by new data-driven services, produces and reconfigures value and economic growth within the creative industries, proposing 'a framework for value creation, centralising

GLAM data in value as co-created and value as the co-creation of meaning' (Terras et al. 2021, 5). While such a reframing of digital cultural heritage content as a resource for economic growth within the creative industries could open a new chapter for the GLAM sector, especially at a time of growing economic crisis and constant shrinking of investment, it also requires an acceptance that

> institutions will no longer be able to control value within data economies. The value of datasets are not predetermined, in a linear value chain, but open to co-creation by others in a value constellation . . . beyond the institutional context. In doing so, it is important to acknowledge the tensions that exist between innovative research and development, community participation and commercial imperatives, particularly in the cultural heritage space. (Terras et al. 2021, 10)

Speaking of the economic value of digital cultural heritage, it is well known that the development and maintenance of digital and born-digital cultural heritage content are costly and labour-intensive processes. What was not available, though, at least back in 2012, was a 'definitive evidence base that could provide concrete numbers about the economic value of digital collections' (Hughes 2012, 7). Almost a decade later, in 2024, a report was commissioned by the Towards a National Collection programme to estimate the Total Economic Value of a future unified digital collection of cultural heritage assets in the UK. Through a contingent valuation study, the report concluded that a Total Economic Value for the service would be £425.5 million, a figure derived from the general population survey results of an average willingness to pay (in terms of an increase in annual taxes) £8.02 per person to support the development, maintenance and free accessibility of a unified digital collection of cultural heritage assets for the UK (Alma Economics 2024, 15). How extensible this methodology is to other national, regional and international contexts remains to be seen.

The evidence gap is gradually being filled, but the landscape in which the value of digital cultural heritage is determined continues to shift. The rise of new technologies – specifically the recent developments in Generative AI – brings both opportunities and challenges in the cultural heritage space, particularly, as mentioned earlier, when it comes to openness and the ethical use of Generative AI. AI transforms how we can work on and with cultural heritage data and enables new forms of computational exploration and analysis. It can also contribute to the shaping of the social and economic value of cultural heritage institutions as trusted sources of data for computational exploration, analysis and synthesis. For example, AI presents an opportunity to enhance and curate digital cultural heritage collections in libraries by facilitating seamless exploration, analysis and interconnection for the research community and the general public (Colavizza et al. 2021; Jaillant 2022; Neudecker 2022). However, AI applications, particularly Generative AI systems predominantly controlled by large commercial entities, present significant ethical and legal challenges that we are only just starting to grapple with. The black-box nature of Generative AI systems exacerbates transparency issues, particularly regarding the sources and copyright status of their training data, while reliance on elite datasets risks excluding marginalised groups and perspectives, reproducing knowledge hierarchies and amplifying inherent biases in the datasets. Important community-based initiatives and communities of practice in the digital cultural heritage field, like Collections-as-Data, AI4LAM[3] and BigLAM,[4] have been actively trying to address current and emerging challenges, while highlighting the heritage community's values of responsibility and care towards the adoption of AI.

Finally, digital cultural heritage is increasingly included in wider discussions of and investigations into the value of heritage and culture broadly defined, but its separateness and difference remain acknowledged. In October 2022, for example, the AHRC and the UK's Department for Digital, Culture, Media and Sport launched a funding opportunity to explore 'Research culture and heritage capital with an interdisciplinary team'. The aim of the programme was to 'help develop a robust and holistic approach for capturing and articulating the value of cultural heritage'.[5] Digital cultural heritage was explicitly acknowledged, but in a separate strand focused on the 'valuation of digital assets'. The guidance for applicants noted that there are further differences between the digitised and the born digital. The concern here is with monetising the value of digital cultural heritage to the public, but the gaps in evidence identified also pertain to other forms of value. Six projects were ultimately funded, of which one was duly focused on digital cultural heritage.[6] 'Valuing digital cultural heritage and assets', led by the University of Portsmouth, aimed to 'apply techniques from behavioural economics to assess the economic and cultural value of digital culture and heritage assets'.[7] It encompassed both the digitised and the born-digital and was concerned with combining qualitative and quantitative data to inform cultural heritage valuation.

Values and ethical challenges

Conceptualising digital cultural heritage as a set of dynamic cultural and social practices and processes around remembering as well as understanding and engaging with the present, rather than a static entity defined solely by its economic or social value, reveals the intricate web of meanings and values inherited by the stakeholders and communities involved. Indeed, processes such as data selection, documentation, representation, interpretation, data visualisation, management and governance, as well as digital tools, innovative technologies, platforms, classification systems and standards used in any aspect and type of digital cultural heritage, are not just abstract concepts or simple checkboxes in a project proposal or a management board; they are amalgams of reflective, insightful, context-specific, dynamic and collaborative decisions and practices and carry a multitude of assumptions, implicit (or explicit) biases, complex dilemmas and, ultimately, deliberate choices. Furthermore, none of these processes and choices will have been adopted or made in a historical, cultural or institutional vacuum. What is digitised, and why? Who is represented in cultural heritage data? Who is missing or not included? What system or standard is being used? Who has made these choices? Of course, these questions are not new, but with digital technologies, and more recently the emergence of large, varied and complex digital datasets as well as advanced, public-facing computational systems and methods, these ethical challenges are even more amplified and pressing (Foka and Griffin 2024).

One way of engaging with ethical challenges and biases in digital cultural heritage collections is through acknowledging them and making them visible and present, instead of attempting to mitigate or eliminate them. Recent scholarship has focused on exploring and highlighting the existence of biased data in digital cultural heritage collections and the reasons behind it (Sever 2020; Kizhner et al. 2021; Ortolja-Baird and Nyhan 2022). Ethical risks are higher for disputed cultural heritage, particularly when its meanings, narratives and values are challenged, or in cases of communities who are historically and continuingly marginalised or, finally, when access to and the enjoyment and benefits of heritage are at risk. Many digital cultural heritage projects and initiatives have attempted to address historical inaccuracies, omissions or biases affecting various communities, including the adoption of the CARE principles (Carroll et al. 2020), as previously discussed. One such example is The Real Face of White Australia, originally called Invisible

Australians,[8] a project that aimed to showcase diversity in early twentieth-century Australia by exploring government records that document the life of Indigenous Australians and non-Europeans in the country, thereby giving digital visibility to their lives and stories. The Museum of British Colonialism, with founding members in Kenya and the UK, has the stated aim of 'exploring suppressed histories' and altering 'the narrative around British colonialism and its legacies'.[9]

Powerful projects and initiatives are increasingly animated by communities to manage their own digital cultural heritage. An important early example is that of the Mukurtu content management system (CMS), 'a grass-roots project aiming to empower communities to manage, share, narrate, and exchange their digital heritage in culturally relevant and ethically-minded ways'.[10] It originated as a collaboration between members of the Warumungu community and researchers at Washington State University to produce a Mukurtu Wumpurrarni-kari Archive. It subsequently developed into an open CMS that allows Indigenous communities to control access to their digital heritage according to cultural protocols. The CMS is structured to allow for the creation and sharing (or not) of multiple narratives associated with digital heritage items, so that communities 'can tell your stories and your history, your way'.[11] It has been used by projects such as the Polynesian Photo Archives[12] at the Feleti Barstow Public Library in American Samoa and Gather,[13] a project that seeks to connect Aboriginal communities with the collections that belong to them but are held in the State Library of New South Wales. As Roopika Risam notes, 'The idea that information wants to be free has been an influential one . . . Yet, this approach to knowledge is grounded in epistemologies of the Global North'. Mukurtu, by contrast, 'embeds Indigenous epistemology into its design' (Risam 2018, 83).

Digital cultural heritage exists within a modern technological landscape marked by significant disparities in access and resources. So, although digital technologies have made access to cultural heritage, data acquisition and reuse potentially quicker and easier, this is not the case for all regions and communities (Kizhner et al. 2021). When source communities are, technologically or geographically, remote from the processes of selecting, presenting and interpreting their own heritage in the digital sphere, there is a risk that the outcomes will reflect the priorities and perspectives of external researchers, practitioners and institutions rather than those of the communities whose heritage is being digitised.

Unlike earlier digital projects concerned with the cultural heritage of the Global South, which often remained within the bounds of academic discourse and employed generalised ethical framings, a number of recent initiatives have taken a more situated and interventionist approach. These efforts not only highlight structural tensions – particularly in the Global South and among non-privileged communities – but also adopt more nuanced, diverse and context-specific frameworks of analysis. Crucially, they seek to move beyond critique towards actionable change, engaging funders and stakeholders in more socially responsive, impact-driven work that bridges research with real-world intervention.

Complementing and extending the work of the Oxford University Heritage Network (OUHN),[14] the Endangered Cultural Heritage in the Global South Hub (ECHGS)[15] provides a vital platform for research into the complex challenges facing cultural heritage in Official Development Assistance (ODA)-eligible countries, particularly in the Middle East and Africa. The Hub places a strong emphasis on the social science dimensions of heritage, critically engaging with the intersections of theory, politics, ethics and technology. It currently facilitates interdisciplinary research on how cultural heritage is created, identified, valued and protected by local populations, experts, international agencies and academics, as well as how it is threatened by conflict, climate change, development and tourism. These concerns are deeply intertwined with longstanding relationships between the Global North and South, making cultural heritage central to current debates around national and international ODA programmes. Recent activities include an international conference in Oxford (July 2025) and planned workshops, all aimed at strengthening networks among Global South and international heritage professionals to foster collaboration, influence policy and empower local communities. ECHGS also provides essential infrastructure to support research and capacity-building in these contexts, serving as a platform for multi-disciplinary collaboration. It acts as a key point of engagement with external stakeholders in both the UK and the Global South, including NGOs, the media, government departments, policymakers, funders and heritage communities (Rouhani 2025).

In a similar vein, a recent British Council report, developed through its long-standing Cultural Protection Fund (CPF) partnership with the UK's Department for Culture, Media and Sport, offers valuable insights into safeguarding cultural heritage at risk from conflict and climate change.

The CPF supports efforts that not only protect heritage but also contribute to sustainable social stability and economic prosperity. Taking the CPF as its foundation, the report draws on the experiences of twenty-five cultural heritage practitioners from Egypt, Ethiopia, Iraq and Kenya. Developed in close collaboration with the CPF community, it reflects both global and local perspectives, with the situated knowledge and innovative practices of contributors playing a central role in shaping its findings. Through its exploration of emerging technologies, cutting-edge case studies and practical recommendations across the digital cultural heritage pipeline, the report aims to support practitioners and funders in embedding technology in ways that are sustainable, inclusive and community led. Crucially, it also provides a foundation for the British Council and other funding bodies to design future programmes grounded in the lived realities and needs of the communities it seeks to serve (McKenna et al. 2025).

Community and professional values

Over the past three decades, the rise of community archives, accompanied by 'community' and 'participatory' turns in archival and memory practices, has opened up a new era for digital cultural heritage. Community archives can give space to previously excluded voices, allowing people to take control of their own histories and share their experiences and memories, developing shared interpretation and understanding (Popple, Prescott and Mutibwa 2020). Digital ecosystems and platforms have become an integral part of these community-driven heritage practices as people from marginalised groups and underrepresented communities, including LGBTQ+ communities, feminist networks, diasporic and Black communities, started to take ownership of their heritage and create their own digital archives, sometimes in collaboration with archivists, heritage professionals and academic researchers, in order to tell their stories and to ensure that the historical record is more representative, inclusive and diverse (Webb 2018; Giglitto et al. 2024). Such frameworks of co-creation and participatory practice in digital cultural heritage are leading to new modes of collaboration, interpretation and engagement around heritage and culture, as well as to a shared understanding of the ownership of and responsibility towards the sustainability and preservation of these vital collections, ensuring the enduring value of the communities and their contributions. An early and highly influential intervention was the set of resources developed by

Documenting the Now, in response to the increasing use of social media to record and respond to historical events. Over time, it has developed 'open-source tools and community-centered practices that support the ethical collection, use, and preservation of publicly available content shared on web and social media'.[16] It works particularly closely with activist groups in the US, helping them to take control of their own archives and determine how and by whom they will be used. Many other initiatives have since focused on this area, for example the 'Community Archives Digital Preservation Toolkit' (Digital Preservation Coalition 2024), which is a key output from the Towards a National Collection 'Our Heritage, Our Stories' project.

Ultimately, reflection on values and ethics in digital cultural heritage helps us to explore and evolve how all stakeholders – including cultural heritage practitioners, researchers and data scientists – can be critically active and self-conscious in their professional practices on a daily basis. This 'ethics as practice' perspective (Rutherford et al. 2024) emphasises enduring values such as respect, trust, empathy and responsibility towards both human and non-human actors, underscoring a commitment to other communities, as well as to the environment. Digital cultural heritage is created and consumed within complex interdisciplinary networks of human production and collaboration, encompassing different forms of knowledge and different kinds of contribution from various stakeholders and professionals. Consequently, it is essential to explore new modes and forms of recognition, evaluation and credit attribution across the field, challenges and practices that have already been widely explored and addressed in digital scholarship and digital humanities (Nowviskie 2012; Graban et al. 2019) through initiatives such as the Contributor Role Taxonomy (CRediT).[17] Following Smith's claim for heritage, digital cultural heritage offers a platform 'through which people can negotiate identity and values and meanings that underlie that, but through which they challenge and attempt to redefine their position or "place" in the world around them' (Smith 2006, 7). It is important to emphasise (re)negotiation and redefinition here, as the values associated with digital cultural heritage are and should not be static or determined by single groups or cultures. Perhaps, however, we can aim for a set of core values for digital cultural heritage that can help 'to tackle the challenges of sustainability, accountability and inclusiveness that are central to [its] long-term societal and cultural worth' (Schafer and Winters 2021, 129), while remaining responsive and adaptable.

Notes

1 Rhizome, described as 'the home of born-digital art and culture since 1996' is affiliated to the New Museum of Contemporary Art in New York, https://rhizome .org/ [accessed 26 September 2024].

2 Europeana Value Lenses, https://europeana.atlassian.net/wiki/spaces/CB /pages/2261712897/Value+Lenses [accessed 30 January 2025].

3 AI4LAM, https://sites.google.com/view/ai4lam [accessed 30 January 2025].

4 BigLAM: BigScience Libraries, Archives and Museums, https://huggingface.co /biglam [accessed 30 January 2025].

5 'Research Culture and Heritage Capital with an Interdisciplinary Team', https: //www.ukri.org/opportunity/research-culture-and-heritage-capital-with-an -interdisciplinary-team/ [accessed 30 January 2025].

6 'AHRC/DCMS Culture and Heritage Capital Research Call – Bid Recipients', https://www.gov.uk/guidance/ahrcdcms-culture-and-heritage-capital-research -call-bid-recipients [accessed 31 July 2025].

7 'New Projects to Measure Value of Culture and Heritage to Society', https: //www.ukri.org/news/new-projects-to-measure-value-of-culture-and-heritage -to-society/ [accessed 31 July 2025].

8 The Real Face of White Australia, http://www.realfaceofwhiteaustralia.net/ [accessed 30 January 2025].

9 The Museum of British Colonialism, https://museumofbritishcolonialism.org /our-work/ [accessed 5 August 2025].

10 Mukurtu CMS, https://mukurtu.org/ [accessed 30 January 2025].

11 Mukurtu CMS, https://mukurtu.org/ [accessed 30 January 2025].

12 Polynesian Photo Archives, http://feletibarstowppa.org/ [accessed 5 August 2025].

13 Gather, https://gather.sl.nsw.gov.au/ [accessed 5 August 2025].

14 Oxford University Heritage Network, https://www.heritagenetwork.ox.ac.uk / [accessed 1 August 2025].

15 Endangered Cultural Heritage in the Global South Hub, https://www.arch.ox .ac.uk/echgs-hub-0#tab-5362806 [accessed 1 August 2025].

16 Documenting the Now, https://www.docnow.io/ [accessed 30 January 2025].

17 Contributor Role Taxonomy (CRediT), https://credit.niso.org/ [accessed 30 January 2025].

Chapter 5

Sustainability and preservation

Digital cultural heritage in danger

As cultural heritage organisations have moved to embed emerging technologies in their strategic visions, systems and services, researchers and cultural heritage professionals have increasingly realised the need for rapid digital and technological adaptation in their practices, methods and decision-making. At the same time, the potential for exploring, analysing and understanding cultural heritage objects in new ways, as well as the challenges arising from and within the adaptation of these technologies, have pushed the boundaries of the ever-changing cultural heritage landscape, including its structural, governance and financial ecosystems. In this context, huge strategic investments in digital research and resources have been put in place, initiating an era of research, experimentation and innovation. For example, since it was founded in 1998, the AHRC has invested 'over £2.5bn in arts and humanities across the UK, supporting jobs, improving skills and focusing support in key strategic areas for the UK's prosperity'.[1] More than £400 million of this investment has been directed towards digital research and innovation. This funding has enabled exciting interdisciplinary explorations in data creation, data management, computational access, storage and long-term preservation, but also in the systems and infrastructures that are built to support them.[2] The impact of this investment in the UK has been huge and it is matched by similar programmes in other Global North countries. The creation of research projects and programmes, knowledge exchange spaces and engagement activities has been driving change across the arts and humanities, cultural heritage and the creative industries while directly addressing the needs of their many audiences.

Although these investments have led to new partnerships and impactful research outputs across the cultural heritage sector, the reliance on short-term grant funding for digital innovation has resulted in major challenges for the sustaining of digital resources even in the short term. Cameron writes that 'while paper-based information may be preserved by benign neglect, digital resources either exist or are lost forever' (Cameron 2021, 30). Or as Neal Beagrie similarly notes:

> in the right conditions papyrus or paper can survive by accident or through benign neglect for centuries, or in the case of the Dead Sea Scrolls, for thousands of years . . . In contrast, digital information will not survive and remain accessible by accident: it requires ongo-ing active management from as early in the life-cycle as possible. (Beagrie 2006, 10)

However, it is important to highlight that the sustainability of digital resources, outputs, systems and infrastructures is not only a discussion about financial or technological decision-making, planning and manage-ment (Tucker 2022). It is also a discussion about human activities (such as key experts losing motivation, moving jobs or retiring and not being replaced) or anti-social human activities (especially hacking and cyber-attacks). Finally, it is a discussion about environmental impact.

In comparison with the often under-resourced public sector, private companies can paradoxically bring a degree of stability and sustainabil-ity. One example of this apparent contradiction is the sudden closure of Jisc Historical Texts. The service has been outlasted by the commercial resources – notably Early English Books Online and Eighteenth Century Collections Online – to which it sought to provide a more cost-effective alternative. A brief news announcement on 29 February 2024, no longer available on the live web, gave subscribing institutions in the UK only five months to arrange alternative purchase and access arrangements for the multiple collections that could previously be accessed through the single Jisc portal (Jisc 2024). It is worth noting that a closure on this scale has an additional impact on the sustainability and rigour of the scholarly ecosystem, in that it is likely to have resulted in numerous broken links in the books and articles that cited material from the Jisc resource.

Innovation and experimentation may be easier in small, relatively agile not-for-profit entities than in more bureaucratic institutions that suffer from persistent under-funding. A particularly interesting approach to the long-term safeguarding of cultural heritage is that of the Flickr Foundation, which has the stated aim that 'One hundred years from now, future generations will have access to the unique visual content available on Flickr today as a result of the Flickr Foundation's efforts to protect and preserve it' (Flickr Foundation n.d.).[3] The Flickr Foundation has developed the concept of the 'data lifeboat' as a means to combat the disappearance of important digital cultural heritage when online services and platforms are closed or collapse: 'A Data Lifeboat is an archival *piece* of Flickr, not *all* of the 50 billion images and their metadata. We envision an archival sliver richer than a mere folder of JPGs: one where you can navigate the content to explore and understand its networked context' (Flickr Foundation n.d.).

The work of the Flickr Foundation is an imaginative response to the challenges of sustaining and preserving content originally hosted by a commercial platform, but it remains something of an outlier. The past three decades are littered with commercial digital services that outgrew their usefulness or were overwhelmed by a competitor. One such is Friends Reunited, launched in 2000, which very quickly became a popular way of getting back in touch with old school friends, to share memories and photos and update them on the progress of your life. It was closed down on 26 February 2016 (Jowitt 2017), and while the company made best efforts to contact its users and give them the opportunity to download their own information, much personal data went with it. In 2019, MySpace announced to its users that it had lost more than a decade's worth of material during a server migration (Hern 2019). The reliance on commercial entities as de facto archives poses a huge danger to the survival of born-digital materials, from the so-called 'sunsetting' of failing services to accidental loss or deliberate erasure. Leaving responsibility for the custodianship of important digital cultural heritage in the hands of businesses that do not have an explicitly archival remit is a huge societal risk.

The MySpace example illustrates the speed with which digital data can disappear and it has become increasingly apparent that even digital archives that have become knitted into the fabric of scholarly and archival infrastructure can be highly vulnerable. Libraries and platforms around the world have been subject to damaging cyber-attacks. On 9 October 2024, for example, the Internet Archive found itself subject to a data breach and Deliberate Denial of Service attack. The hackers inserted a pop-up message on the site that asked: 'Have you ever felt like the Internet Archive runs on sticks and is constantly on the verge of suffering a catastrophic security breach?' (Davis 2024). The Internet Archive restored functionality relatively quickly, including to the Wayback Machine, but this was a sharp reminder of the fragility of digital systems and infrastructure as well as digital archives. In this instance, fortunately, the content of the web archive itself was not accessed. But the hacking of digital archives, the changing of the record, is something that has to be planned for.

Recent British history has shown that even the most well-established cultural institutions can be vulnerable to such bad actors, as anti-social cyber/human activities disrupted most services and activities at The British Library. In October 2023 Rhysida, a hacker group, attacked the online information systems of the library, demanding a ransom of 20 bitcoin, at the time worth around £596,000, to restore services and return the stolen data (British Library 2024a). When the British Library did not agree to pay this ransom, Rhysida publicly released approximately 600GB of leaked material online (Adams 2023). The attack led to the disruption of most library services for months, with some being entirely or partially unavailable for long periods (for example, it was only three months after the attack that the British Library catalogue became available in a read-only format) (British Library 2024b). At the time of writing, almost two years after the attack, the vast UK Web Archive remains inaccessible, its data intact but the infrastructure to deliver it critically damaged.

The vulnerability of the means to find and access digital archives introduces an additional layer of risk. The use of shortened URLs to link to online content became common as a means of saving character space on social media platforms or of presenting a tidier, more readable reference than a long string of characters generated by a database. The URL shortener is now built into much social media, automatically truncating what the user may have pasted in to their post. In July 2024, Google announced that it would be turning off its URL shortener, having previously announced the deprecation of the service in 2018. The blog post where the announcement was made notes that 'Over time, these . . . URLs saw less and less traffic as the years went on – in fact more than 99% of them had no activity in the last month' (Chandel and Babu 2024). But that means that a little under 1 per cent did have activity, and in any case current attention is not a proxy for archival value. Digital pathways can disappear in the same way as data, leaving a landscape strewn with error messages – 'page not found'.

The coincidence of the attacks on the British Library and Internet Archive (Bridge and Zoledziowski 2024) in 2023–4 highlighted the importance and urgency of designing and building stable, secure, safe and sustainable infrastructure, systems and services for accessing digital resources across cultural heritage and information-holding institutions. In order to ensure that digital resources will remain authentic and accessible in the future to anyone who needs them, information-holding institutions (such as the National Health Service[4] and Office for National Statistics[5] in the UK) and large-scale national programmes (such as Smart Data Research UK)[6] have started investing resources in building Safe and Trusted Environments for safe and secure access to data. As these services rely not only on physical and human infrastructures but also on cloud-based and other networked storage systems, environmental sustainability becomes central to conversations about the use of raw materials and the energy that these infrastructures require.

It is perhaps worth unpicking some of the differences between preservation and sustainability and considering that in some cases a particular project or output may, and perhaps should not, be sustained for a long period after the lifetime of its funding. The Endings Project is particularly useful here in its consideration of practical solutions to address the fact that 'our ability to produce digital information continues to outpace our capacity to preserve and access that knowledge for the long haul' (The Endings Project Team n.d.). The project distinguishes five elements of digital projects – data, documentation, processing, products and release management – and highlights the complex interplay between them in the context of sustainability and archiving. It notes that 'code is not expected to have significant longevity' and introduces notions of 'graceful failure' for products such as interfaces and websites. Careful planning from the outset of a project can maximise the chances of sustaining both cultural heritage data and a specific means of access to it, but the data itself is key. 'Digital cultural heritage operates as a dispersed dynamic assemblage of entangled elements and forces' (Cameron 2021, 41) and while all of these can be identified and acknowledged, they cannot always be preserved.

Devising a framework that promotes and supports archiving and preservation that is 'good enough', which moves away from decades of work to develop best practice in relation to digital preservation, is a challenge for cultural heritage practitioners. It is also a challenge for researcher expectations about the representativeness and completeness of collections, or indeed the ease and readiness of access (Goudarouli et al. 2023). The required repositioning is made even more difficult because we are confronted with the loss of digital cultural heritage in real time. To look at the archives of the early web, for example, is to be faced immediately with what we no longer have. The text of a page may have been captured, but perhaps the images are missing, represented only by a symbol of brokenness. As you try to navigate through an archived website using the Wayback Machine, it is often not long before you are faced with the friendly message: 'Hrm. The Wayback Machine has not archived that URL'. Research undertaken by the Pew Research Center revealed that, as of October 2023, 25 per cent of web pages that had existed at some time between 2013 and 2023 were no longer extant on the live web (Rivero et al. 2024). A study of seven million scholarly journals published digitally revealed what is described by Martin Paul Eve as 'an alarming preservation deficit', with almost 28 per cent of the sample 'seemingly unpreserved' (Eve 2024). Born-digital cultural heritage might appear to be slipping through our collective fingers.

There are numerous, well-documented examples of loss arising from the early years of mass digitisation. One of the best known in the UK concerns the heritage digitisation supported by investment from the New Opportunities Fund, which ran from 1999 to 2003. Funding of £50m was available for the digitisation programme (NOF-digi), from a wider budget of £230m for the creation of a People's Network of ICT learning centres in UK public libraries (Woodhouse 2001). References to the programme persist in the UK Government Web Archive in press releases and annual reports, while the last capture of the NOF-digi website accessible via the Wayback Machine dates from 31 March 2005. The next capture of the URL, dating from 18 August 2007, reveals that the domain name had expired a week earlier on 11 August.[7] In terms of the funded projects themselves, as of March 2009 almost a quarter were no longer available online (Jisc 2009), despite evident keen attention paid to the relationship between ease of use, open standards and preservation (Kelly et al. n.d.). Dunning suggested that 'the feeling that the programme was something of a wasted opportunity; digitisation was a complex problem that needed much sophisticated strategic thinking before there could be a serious injection of further public funds' potentially had a chilling effect on further public investment in the digitisation of cultural heritage (Dunning 2009). The history of NOF-digitise is not an easy one to reconstruct, reflecting an all-too-common failure by public bodies and cultural heritage institutions to record and preserve the stories of their digitisation and digitalisation. There is much scope for recovering this important aspect of digital cultural heritage through archival research in combination with oral histories. This is in stark contrast to the extensive coverage of philanthropic and commercial initiatives in this space, notably Google Books (see, for example, Somers 2017; Marcum and Schonfeld 2021; Milligan 2024).

So far, so bad? A sense of a looming crisis in preservation and sustainability is reinforced by the Global 'Bit List' of Endangered Digital Species, published by the Digital Preservation Coalition and revised every two years. Among the types of digital cultural heritage listed as 'practically extinct' are 'Shutdown or Discontinued Video Games', 'Pre-WWW Videotext Data Services and Bulletin Board Services' and 'Non-standard Public Records', by which is meant 'Records created in the course of public administration and subject to public records legislation but created on unofficial channels and platforms and therefore subject to unlawful destruction whether by accident or design'. The 'critically endangered' category includes a range of digital archives, including those of community groups, music production and public enquiries and commissions. There is a notable trend towards increased risk of loss between revisions of the Bit-List and new categories of endangered heritage are regularly added (Digital Preservation Coalition n.d.).

But is this an overly gloomy picture of loss and decay, of ever-growing failure in relation to preservation and sustainability? Ian Milligan argues that 'If, in the mid-1990s, commentators worried about a "digital dark age", we are now in an age of historical abundance', with memory institutions playing a crucial and leading role (Milligan 2024, 1). Digital data is being created and archived in vast quantities – petabytes of text, image, sound and video. Abundance comes with its own challenges, of course, for both archivists and researchers. How do you even begin to identify what an archive of seventy petabytes contains? What use is the now ubiquitous keyword searching, when looking for more or less any term will generate tens of thousands of results? How can individuals and their personal data be protected at this scale? But the fact remains that we already have more data than we quite know what to do with. This is a story of success, of quick action and the ingenuity of memory institutions and archivists, often working with very limited resources.

These apparently competing narratives swirl around born-digital cultural heritage, but they are far from mutually exclusive. We can exist in an environment of both digital abundance and loss, and indeed move from one to the other. Attention to loss and the mitigation of risk is essential if a balance is to be maintained between scarcity and abundance, between ephemerality and long-term preservation and sustainability. The stories of loss and destruction that have tended to dominate discussion overlook the diverse communities that have mobilised to identify, capture, archive, publish and preserve the digital record. This work is happening in cultural heritage institutions; it is happening in communities; it is being carried out by activist and volunteer groups; and it is being undertaken by individuals who either recognise the value of their own digital data or are collecting born-digital material for personal research. Very often it is happening collaboratively, with a cross-sectoral and interdisciplinary openness that is highly unusual. An early recognition of the challenges of securing and preserving digital cultural heritage – whether they arise from abundance or fragility – has brought together archivists, librarians, curators, digital preservation specialists, researchers and technicians to ensure that at least some of our digital past and present persist into the digital future. A striking example of what can be achieved is Saving Ukrainian Cultural Heritage Online (SUCHO), an initiative of over 1,500 international volunteers collaborating online to digitise Ukrainian cultural heritage at risk from war. Their efforts have included archiving more than 5,000 websites and 50TB of data from Ukrainian cultural institutions in order to prevent these websites from going offline and/or being permanently lost.[8]

There is an important caveat to be made, however: the archiving and preservation of digital cultural heritage is an activity overwhelmingly in, by and for the Global North. Data abundance is not a challenge faced by all regions of the world equally; nor is there equality of access to digital cultural heritage. So long as this remains the case, what is preserved and sustained offers only a partial view of the world's heritage, tangible and intangible.

Sustainability planning in digital cultural heritage extends beyond mere technological obsolescence considerations to encompass a dynamic network of 'infrastructures, people, financial, and managerial decisions that are performing a constant tug-of-war with one another while battling about the longevity of digital outputs' (Sichani 2022, 318). It is necessary to approach systems and infrastructures 'as a human and community asset in need of maintenance and support, rather than a technical artefact in need of service management' (Smithies et al. 2019, para 20). By paying attention to the human-intensive nature of digital projects, aspects of skills development, capacity building and inclusivity, as well as continuous user/

community engagement and aspects of legacy management, can be considered as key factors in sustainability planning (Edmond and Morselli 2020).

Environmental concerns

Moving from digital and technological fragility to the environmental aspect of sustainability, one may wonder how unwelcome the technological obsolescence of digital infrastructure is in the context of an environmental crisis. In our everyday lives, we generate vast amounts of digital garbage, including outdated hardware, obsolete devices and unused data. E-waste pollution has long been recognised as the flip side of digital preservation efforts for born-digital cultural assets, and is just one of the environmental challenges intertwined with the digital age. What might now be required is a 'paradigm shift in digital preservation practice in the areas of appraisal, permanence, and availability' (Pendergrass et al. 2019, 165).

The environmental impact of digital cultural heritage content is not limited to its end-of-life but extends throughout its usage. GLAM institutions rely heavily on information and communication technology, involving networks, hardware and software, not only when archiving digital content but also when providing access to their digital holdings. Doing anything with digital data – whether digitisation, data acquisition, documentation, processing, visualisation, archiving, modelling, developing 3D models and virtual reality experiences or devising digital forms of public engagement via social media or online streaming – involves using energy, storage, hardware and software. And there is always an environmental cost that is almost invisible to those of us asking for access to more datasets or commissioning new forms of advanced analysis through machine learning, that is, energy consumption in power-hungry data centres and networks, often powered by non-renewable energy sources. The more digital data we generate, store and use, the more the environmental impact of our endeavours intensifies. Advanced digital processes, including AI systems, create and use even more data, which requires greater energy for storage, processing and reuse, leading to a vicious cycle of increasingly detrimental impact on the environment. In particular, Generative AI systems face a critical 'energy problem' due to the significant computational demands at every stage of their lifecycle, from training models and fine-tuning to computing resources and energy-intensive infrastructure, including data centres (Bashir et al. 2024). The figures speak for themselves and the news is not promising: the technology sector could produce 14 per cent of global emissions by 2040 (*The Guardian* 2017) and the data centre industry (employed by major players such as Microsoft Azure, Google Cloud or Amazon Web Services (AWS)) is responsible for 2–3 per cent of global greenhouse gas emissions.[9] Finally, the International Energy Agency predicts that energy consumption by data centres will double between 2022 and 2026, reaching 1,000 TWh – approximately equivalent to Japan's total energy usage[10] – while the global volume of stored data doubles every four years.[11] Questions of value, as discussed in Chapter 4, become even more pressing when these are the consequences of high computation and ever-increasing data volumes.

Lastly, it is crucial to recognise that the environmental impact of digital technologies reflects deep-rooted and inequitable financial dynamics. The technological advancements of the Global North have caused significant environmental and human costs, particularly in socio-economically vulnerable areas of the Global South, reminding us that the climate impact of these technologies tells 'a dark tale of colonialism, genocide, devastated ecologies, toxicity, extinctions, and a shameful legacy that will take more than decades to make right' (Cubitt 2017, 10).

The UK is committed to reaching Net Zero by 2050, which means that total greenhouse gas emissions would be equal to the emissions removed from the atmosphere, with the aim of limiting global warming and resultant climate change.[12] The EU also has a goal to be climate-neutral by 2050 with net-zero greenhouse gas emissions, an objective at the heart of the European Green Deal, and a legally binding target thanks to the European Climate Law, on top of national long-term strategies.[13] However, environmental concerns and sustainability strategies are often overlooked in digital cultural heritage contexts, and when they are considered, they tend to be treated as an afterthought, focused on managing legacy projects in need of repair, obsolete infrastructures or devices and existing data in need of maintenance (Richardson 2022). These issues should instead be approached as strategic, long-term considerations, essential for sustainability. It is to be hoped that the national and international strategic commitments towards a transition to a climate-neutral society will be viewed as an opportunity and indeed urgent requirement for researchers and cultural heritage professionals to adopt more environmentally sustainable methods, approaches and decision-making processes that place sustainability frameworks at the centre of their practice. There will be a key role for initiatives such as the Climate Heritage Network (CHN), whose manifesto and action plan aim to bring together GLAMs, government agencies, NGOs, universities, businesses and other organisations committed to encouraging greater synergistic collaboration on climate action to re-orient climate policy, planning and action at all levels to account for every dimension of culture, from arts to heritage (Climate Heritage Network n.d.). Aiding professional bodies and research institutions in their ambitions to achieve Net Zero means that plans and frameworks should be in place that address the act of not preserving, and consequently of discontinuing, access to digital cultural heritage, in a world where human impact on the environment needs to be carefully monitored and regulated.

Notes

1 Arts and Humanities Research Council 25 Years of Excellence and Impact, https://www.discover.ukri.org/AHRC-impact/index.html [accessed 1 August 2025].

2 UKRI Digital Research Infrastructure Programme, https://www.ukri.org/what-we-do/creating-world-class-research-and-innovation-infrastructure/digital-research-infrastructure/; 'Major Research and Innovation Infrastructure Investment Announced', https://www.ukri.org/news/major-research-and-innovation-infrastructure-investment-announced/ [accessed 1 August 2025].

3 Flickr is a video- and image-sharing service, whose Flickr Commons was often used as a platform for the dissemination of image collections by cultural heritage institutions, https://www.flickr.com/ [accessed 1 August 2025].

4 'Trusted Research Environment Service for England', https://digital.nhs.uk/services/trusted-research-environment-service-for-england [accessed 30 January 2025].

5 Integrated Data Service, https://integrateddataservice.gov.uk/ [accessed 30 January 2025].

6 Smart Data Research UK, https://www.sdruk.ukri.org/about-smart-data-research/ [accessed 30 January 2025].

7 Interestingly, this is not the end of the story. A 10 May 2010 capture of the URL reveals a NOF-digitise home page bearing a copyright date of 2009. It had disappeared again by 10 January 2016.

8 SUCHO, https://www.sucho.org/ [accessed 30 January 2025].

9 'Data Centres and Data Transmission Networks', https://www.iea.org/energy-system/buildings/data-centres-and-data-transmission-networks#tracking [accessed 30 January 2025].

10 'Electricity 2024: Executive Summary', https://www.iea.org/reports/electricity-2024/executive-summary [accessed 30 January 2025].

11 'Big Data Statistics: How Much Data is There in the World?' https://rivery.io
/blog/big-data-statistics-how-much-data-is-there-in-the-world/ [accessed 30
January 2025].

12 'The UK's Plans and Progress to Reach Net Zero by 2050', https:
//commonslibrary.parliament.uk/research-briefings/cbp-9888/ [accessed
30 January 2025].

13 '2050 Long-Term Strategy', https://climate.ec.europa.eu/eu-action/climate
-strategies-targets/2050-long-term-strategy_en [accessed 30 January 2025].

Chapter 6

Conclusion

In the preceding chapters, we have aimed to explore the meanings and contexts of 'digital cultural heritage', through the lenses of access, use and reuse, value(s), and the sustainability and preservation of cultural heritage collections. We have, of course, considered the collections held by memory and information-holding institutions, but we have also been concerned with digitised cultural heritage that exists in other settings, from community archives to commercial entities. We have attempted to outline the scope of what constitutes digital cultural heritage – and what the concept might evolve to include in the future. While we may have gone some way to achieving breadth, there will inevitably be areas to which we have not paid due attention or that fall outside our collective expertise. If breadth of focus is within grasp, this short book is certainly not designed to go into any one aspect of digital cultural heritage in depth. It aims for survey and synthesis rather than detailed exploration; to spark conversation and even create challenge; to serve as a catalyst for further research. It is a partial view of a particular moment in time.

We have brought together key concepts, projects, initiatives, policies and frameworks to inform discussion about the multiple interpretations, contexts and uses of what may constitute 'digital cultural heritage'. To conclude as we began, we have sought to think about how we got here, what 'here' looks like – depending on your vantage point – and how the landscape of digital cultural heritage may develop in years to come. We have been concerned with the past, present and possible futures of digital cultural heritage, all of which remain underexplored and/or contested in important aspects. The book foregrounds examples that demonstrate the parameters of digital cultural heritage today, exploring the current landscapes of research and practice, identifying some of the different human and technical factors that are shaping those landscapes, reflecting on the ambiguous and mutating forms of digital cultural heritage, and identifying possible future areas for research.

We hope that this volume will serve as something of a call to action. First, it is a call to recognise the value of the myriad forms of digital cultural heritage, from a digitised version of a unique medieval Book of Hours, to a discussion thread on the social media platform Bluesky, to the contents of a government email server. We may not be able to fully define value, but we can begin to look for it beyond the traditional locations, to integrate the digital into wider national and international discussions about heritage and culture. Second, it is a call for increased attention to and investment in the human and technical infrastructures that allow the collection, preservation and presentation of digital cultural heritage. Within a generally under-resourced sector, the teams and individuals entrusted with safeguarding digital forms of cultural heritage are often among those facing the greatest constraints. Digital cultural heritage, as distinct from digital education and engagement, for example, is frequently either an add-on to core business or simply a step that is altogether too far for smaller institutions and organisations. Finally, it is a call for increased collaboration and dialogue between all of those who have a stake in the futures of digital cultural heritage. As noted elsewhere in this book, openness to collaboration has been one of the hallmarks of the field, but there is scope for greater dialogue and partnership, both cross-sectoral and interdisciplinary. For collaboration to thrive, however, institutions need to foster an environment in which there is time and space for experimentation and conversation. We hope that others will follow the example of this book, which is co-authored by researchers working in higher education and cultural heritage and aims to speak to both sectors. It is a small step, but an important one.

The consequences of not working across boundaries – of all kinds – to identify and safeguard digital cultural heritage are serious and the pressures on time and resources are growing. Digital materials are vulnerable; even the most apparently secure can disappear with little or no warning. We cannot, and should not, keep everything, but we need to understand the 'contours' (Ahnert et al. 2023, 34) of the digital cultural heritage that is being created around us every day in order to focus limited resources, marshal scarce skills and direct energy and key expertise. It is a crucial work in progress.

Bibliography

Adams, Geraldine Kendall. 2023. 'Museums on Alert Following British Library Cyber Attack'. Museums Association. 20 December 2023. Accessed 24 November 2025. https://www.museumsassociation .org/museums-journal/news/2023/12/museums-on-alert-following -british-library-cyber-attack/.

Agosti, Maristella, Nicola Orio and Chiara Ponchia. 2018. 'Promoting User Engagement with Digital Cultural Heritage Collections'. *International Journal on Digital Libraries* 19 (4): 353–66. https://doi .org/10.1007/s00799-018-0245-y.

Ahnert, Ruth, Emma Griffin, Mia Ridge and Giorgia Tolfo. 2023. *Collaborative Historical Research in the Age of Big Data*. Cambridge: Cambridge University Press.

Alkemade, Henk, Steven Claeyssens, Giovanni Colavizza, Nuno Freire, Jörg Lehmann, Clemens Neudecker, Giulia Osti and Daniel van Strien. 2023. 'Datasheets for Digital Cultural Heritage Datasets'. *Journal of Open Humanities Data* 9 (1): 17. https://doi.org/10.5334/johd.124.

Alma Economics. 2024. 'Towards a National Collection: Total Economic Value of a Unified Digital Collection'. Towards a National Collection. https://doi.org/10.5281/zenodo.12755041.

Ames, Sarah and Lucy Havens. 2022. 'Exploring National Library of Scotland Datasets with Jupyter Notebooks'. *IFLA Journal* 48 (1): 50–56. https://doi.org/10.1177/03400352211065484.

Anderson, Benedict. 1983. *Imagined Communities. Reflections on the Origin and Spread of Nationalism*. London: Verso.

Assmann, Jan. 2008. 'Communicative and Cultural Memory'. In *Cultural Memory Studies: An International and Interdisciplinary Handbook*, edited by Astrid Erll and Ansgar Nünning, 109–18. Berlin, New York: Walter de Gruyter.

Azzopardi, Elaine, Jasper O. Kenter, Juliette Young, Chris Leakey, Seb O'Connor, Simone Martino, Wesley Flannery et al. 2023. 'What Are Heritage Values? Integrating Natural and Cultural Heritage into Environmental Valuation'. *People and Nature* 5 (2): 368–83. https: //doi.org/10.1002/pan3.10386.

Bailey-Ross, Claire, Steven Gray, Jack Ashby, Melissa Terras, Andrew Hudson-Smith and Claire Warwick. 2017. 'Engaging the Museum Space: Mobilizing Visitor Engagement with Digital Content Creation'. *Digital Scholarship in the Humanities* 32 (4): 689–708. https://doi.org/10.1093/llc/fqw041.

Bashir, Noman, Priya Donti, James Cuff, Sydney Sroka, Marija Ilic, Vivienne Sze, Christina Delimitrou and Elsa Olivetti. 2024. 'The Climate and Sustainability Implications of Generative AI'. *An MIT Exploration of Generative AI*, March 2024. Accessed 24 November 2025. https://mit-genai.pubpub.org/pub/8ulgrckc/release/2.

Beagrie, Neil. 2006. 'Digital Curation for Science, Digital Libraries, and Individuals'. *International Journal of Digital Curation* 1: 3–16. https://doi.org/10.2218/ijdc.v1i1.2.

Beel, David and Claire Wallace. 2020. 'Gathering Together: Social Capital, Cultural Capital and the Value of Cultural Heritage in a Digital Age'. *Social & Cultural Geography* 21 (5): 3, 697–717. https://doi.org/10.1080/14649365.2018.1500632.

Ben-David, Anat. 2021. 'Critical Web Archive Research'. In *The Past Web: Exploring Web Archives*, edited by Daniel Gomes, Elena Demidova, Jane Winters and Thomas Risse, 181–8. Cham: Springer International Publishing. https://doi.org/10.1007/978-3-030-63291-5_14.

Benardou, Agiatis, Erik Champion, Costis Dallas and Lorna Hughes, eds. 2019. *Cultural Heritage Infrastructures in Digital Humanities*. Abingdon: Routledge.

Bikakis, Antonis, Eero Hyvönen, Stéphane Jean, Béatrice Markhoff and Alessandro Mosca. 2021. 'Editorial: Special Issue on Semantic Web for Cultural Heritage'. *Semantic Web* 12 (2): 163–7. https://doi.org/10.3233/SW-210425.

Bonacchi, Chiara and Marta Krzyzanska. 2019. 'Digital Heritage Research Re-Theorised: Ontologies and Epistemologies in a World of Big Data'. *International Journal of Heritage Studies* 25 (12): 1235–47. https://doi.org/10.1080/13527258.2019.1578989.

Boyle, James. 2009. 'A Copyright Black Hole Swallows Our Culture'. *Financial Times*, September 2009. Accessed 24 November 2025. https://www.ft.com/content/6811a9d4-9b0f-11de-a3a1-00144feabdc0.

Bridge, Sarah and Anya Zoledziowski. 2024. '1 Million Books and 4 Months Later, Toronto's Library Recovers from a Cyberattack'. *CBC*

News, 27 February 2024. Accessed 24 November 2025. https://www
.cbc.ca/news/canada/toronto/toronto-library-ransomware-recovery
-1.7126412.

British Library. 2024a. 'Learning Lessons from the Cyber-Attack: British
Library Cyber Incident Review'. Accessed 24 November 2025. https:
//www.bl.uk/home/british-library-cyber-incident-review-8-march
-2024.pdf/.

British Library. 2024b. 'Restoring Our Services: Update'. 30 July 2024.
Accessed 24 November 2025. https://blogs.bl.uk/living-knowledge
/2024/07/restoring-our-services-30-july-2024-update-.html.

British Library. n.d. 'British Library x British Fashion Council Student
Fashion Awards'. Accessed 17 September 2024. https://blogs.bl.uk
/digital-scholarship/2021/03/british-library-x-british-fashion-council
-student-fashion-awards.html.

BrodeFrank, Jessica. 2024. 'Strengthening Digital Engagement to
Provide Intersectional Narratives within Museums Using User
Generated Metadata: A Case Study at Chicago's Adler Planetarium
and the Applications Beyond'. PhD thesis, University of London.
Accessed 24 November 2025. https://sas-space.sas.ac.uk/9826/.

Brown, Kathryn. 2024. 'After Art History? Artworks as Data'. *The Art
Bulletin*, 106 (2): 33–6. Accessed 24 November 2025. https://www
.tandfonline.com/doi/abs/10.1080/00043079.2024.2296277.

Bunout, Estelle, Maud Ehrmann and Frédéric Clavert, eds. 2023.
*Digitised Newspapers: A New Eldorado for Historians? Reflections on
Tools, Methods and Epistemology*. Munich: De Gruyter Oldenbourg.
https://doi.org/10.1515/9783110729214.

Burke, Verity, Dolly Jørgensen and Finn Arne Jørgensen. 2020.
'Museums at Home: Digital Initiatives in Response to COVID-19'. *Norsk
Museumstidsskrift* 16 (2): 117–23.

Butler, Beverley. 2006. 'Heritage and the Present Past'. In *The
Handbook of Material Culture*, edited by Christopher Tilley, Webb
Keane and Susanne Kuechler-Fogden, 463–79. London: Sage
Publications.

Cameron, Fiona R. 2021. *The Future of Digital Data, Heritage
and Curation: In a More-Than-Human World*. Oxford: Taylor &
Francis, 3–4–61.

Cameron, Fiona and Sarah Kenderdine. 2007. *Theorizing Digital Cultural
Heritage: A Critical Discourse*. Cambridge, MA: MIT Press.

Candela, Gustavo, Sally Chambers and Tim Sherratt. 2023. 'An Approach to Assess the Quality of Jupyter Projects Published by GLAM Institutions'. *Journal of the Association for Information Science and Technology* 74 (13): 1550–64. https://doi.org/10.1002/asi.24835.

Candela, Gustavo, María Dolores Sáez, Pilar Escobar and Manuel Marco-Such. 2020. 'Reusing Digital Collections from GLAM Institutions'. *Journal of Information Science*, 48 (2): 251–67. https://doi.org/10.1177/0165551520950246.

Cannelli, Beatrice. 2024. 'Archiving Social Media: A Comparative Study of the Practices, Obstacles, and Opportunities Related to the Development of Social Media Archives'. PhD thesis, University of London. Accessed 5 January 2026. https://sas-space.sas.ac.uk/10023/.

Capurro, Carlotta and Marta Severo. 2023. 'Mapping European Digital Heritage Politics: An Empirical Study of Europeana as a Web-Based Network'. *Heritage & Society*: 1–21. https://doi.org/10.1080/2159032X.2023.2266801.

Carroll, Stephanie Russo, Ibrahim Garba, Oscar L. Figueroa-Rodríguez, Jarita Holbrook, Raymond Lovett, Simeon Materechera, Mark Parsons et al. 2020. 'The CARE Principles for Indigenous Data Governance'. *Data Science Journal* 19 (1). https://doi.org/10.5334/dsj-2020-043.

Carroll, Stephanie Russo, Edit Herczog, Maui Hudson, Keith Russell and Shelley Stall. 2021. 'Operationalizing the CARE and FAIR Principles for Indigenous Data Futures'. *Scientific Data* 8 (1): 108. https://doi.org/10.1038/s41597-021-00892-0.

Chandel, Sumit and Eldhose Mathokkil Babu. 2024. 'Google URL Shortener Links Will No Longer Be Available: Google Developers Blog'. Accessed 24 November 2025. https://developers.googleblog.com/en/google-url-shortener-links-will-no-longer-be-available/.

CIDOC CRM. n.d. 'What is the CIDOC CRM'. Accessed 24 November 2025. http://cidoc.ics.forth.gr/index.html.

Climate Heritage Network. n.d. Accessed 31 January 2025. https://www.climateheritage.org.

Colavizza, Giovanni, Tobias Blanke, Charles Jeurgens and Julia Noordegraaf. 2021. 'Archives and AI: An Overview of Current Debates and Future Perspectives'. *Journal on Computing and Cultural Heritage* 15 (1): 4:1–4:15. https://doi.org/10.1145/3479010.

Council of Europe. n.d. 'Understanding the Impact of Digitisation on Culture'. Culture and Cultural Heritage. Accessed 24 November 2025.

https://www.coe.int/en/web/culture-and-heritage/culture-and
-digitisation.

Creative Commons. n.d.-a. 'CC Search Portal'. Accessed
17 September 2024. https://search.creativecommons.org/.

Creative Commons. n.d.-b. 'CC0'. Accessed 4 September 2024. https:
//creativecommons.org/public-domain/cc0/.

Creative Commons. n.d.-c. 'Who We Are'. Accessed 4 September 2024.
https://creativecommons.org/mission/.

Cubitt, Sean. 2017. *Finite Media: Environmental Implications of Digital
Technologies*. Durham, NC: Duke University Press. https://doi.org/10
.1215/9780822373476.

Dalbello, Marija. 2009. 'Digital Cultural Heritage: Concepts, Projects, and
Emerging Constructions of Heritage'. In *Proceedings of the Libraries
in the Digital Age*. Accessed 16 December 2025. https://repository
.arizona.edu/handle/10150/106136.

Davis, Wes. 2024. 'The Internet Archive Is under Attack, with a Breach
Revealing Info for 31 Million Accounts'. *The Verge*. Accessed
24 November 2025. https://www.theverge.com/2024/10/9/24266419
/internet-archive-ddos-attack-pop-up-message.

Department for Culture, Media and Sport. 2016. 'The Culture White
Paper: Presented to Parliament by the Secretary of State for Culture,
Media & Sport by Command of Her Majesty'. London. Accessed
16 December 2025. https://assets.publishing.service.gov.uk/media
/5a74fbd0ed915d502d6cc94b/DCMS_The_Culture_White_Paper
_3_.pdf.

Department for Digital, Culture, Media and Sport. 2018. 'The Culture
Is Digital Report'. Accessed 16 December 2025. https://assets
.publishing.service.gov.uk/media/5aa68f84e5274a3e3603a65e/TT
_v4.pdf.

Digital Preservation Coalition. 2024. 'Community Archives Digital
Preservation Toolkit: Digital Preservation Coalition'. Accessed
16 December 2025. https://doi.org/10.7207/communitytoolkit
24-01.

Digital Preservation Coalition. n.d. 'The Global "Bit List" of Endangered
Digital Species'. Accessed 20 September 2024. https://www
.dpconline.org/digipres/champion-digital-preservation/bit-list.

Dryden, Jean. 2024. 'ICA's Copyright Advocacy Work at the World
Intellectual Property Organization'. ICA. 23 April 2024. Accessed

16 December 2025. https://www.ica.org/icas-copyright-advocacy
-work-at-the-world-intellectual-property-organization/.

Dunning, Alastair. 2009. 'Digitising the Past: Next Steps for Public-
Sector Digitisation'. In *Digital Information: Order or Anarchy?* edited
by Lorraine Estelle and Hazel Woodward. London: Facet Publishing.
Accessed 16 December 2025. http://eprints.rclis.org/18048/.

Edmond, Jennifer and Francesca Morselli. 2020. 'Sustainability of Digital
Humanities Projects as a Publication and Documentation Challenge'.
Journal of Documentation 76 (5): 1019–31. https://doi.org/10.1108/JD
-12-2019-0232.

The Endings Project Team. n.d. 'Building Sustainable Digital Humanities
Projects'. Accessed 24 September 2024. https://endings.uvic.ca/.

European Commission. 2019. 'DigitalYou - Digital Culture : Europeana:
Digitised Cultural Archives, with over 53 million items'. 3 April 2019.
Accessed 16 December 2025. https://digital-strategy.ec.europa.eu/en
/news/digitalyou-digital-culture.

European Commission. 2021. 'Digital Cultural Heritage Policy'.
10 November 2021. Accessed 16 December 2025. https://digital-strat
egy.ec.europa.eu/en/policies/cultural-heritage.

Europeana Impact Playbook. 'Introduction: What is Impact?' 2017.
Accessed 16 December 2025. https://europeana.atlassian.net/wiki
/spaces/CB/overview?homepageId=2256699653.

Evans, Jason and Simon Cobb. 2016. 'How the World's First Wikidata
Visiting Scholar Created Linked Open Data for Five Thousand Works of
Art'. *Diff* (blog). 5 November 2016. Accessed 16 December 2025. https:
//diff.wikimedia.org/2016/11/05/wikidata-visiting-scholar-art-dataset/.

Eve, Martin Paul. 2024. 'Digital Scholarly Journals Are Poorly Preserved:
A Study of 7 Million Articles'. *Journal of Librarianship and Scholarly
Communication* 12 (1). https://doi.org/10.31274/jlsc.16288.

Fisher, Katherine. 2021. 'Copyright and Preservation of Born-Digital
Materials: Persistent Challenges and Selected Strategies'. *The
American Archivist* 83 (2): 238–67. https://doi.org/10.17723/0360-9081
-83.2.238.

Flickr Foundation. n.d. 'Data Lifeboat'. Accessed 30 August 2024. https:
//www.flickr.org/programs/content-mobility/data-lifeboat/.

Foka, Anna and Gabriele Griffin. 2024. 'AI, Cultural Heritage, and Bias:
Some Key Queries That Arise from the Use of GenAI'. *Heritage* 7 (11):
6125–36. https://doi.org/10.3390/heritage7110287.

Giaccardi, Elisa. 2012. *Heritage and Social Media: Understanding Heritage in a Participatory Culture*. Abingdon: Routledge.

Giglitto, Danilo, Luigina Ciolfi, Eleanor Lockley and Eirini Kaldeli. 2024. *Digital Approaches to Inclusion and Participation in Cultural Heritage: Insights from Research and Practice in Europe*. Abingdon: Routledge.

Ginzarly, Manal and F. Jordan Srour. 2022. 'Cultural Heritage through the Lens of COVID-19'. *Poetics* 92 (June): 3. https://doi.org/10.1016/j.poetic.2021.101622.

GO FAIR. n.d. 'FAIR Principles'. Accessed 17 September 2024. https://www.go-fair.org/fair-principles/.

Gomes, Daniel, André L. Santos and Mário J. Silva. 2006. 'Managing Duplicates in a Web Archive'. In *Proceedings of the 2006 ACM Symposium on Applied Computing*, 818–25. Dijon, France: ACM. https://doi.org/10.1145/1141277.1141465.

Gosling, Kevin, Gordon McKenna and Adrian Cooper. 2022. 'Digital Collections Audit'. https://doi.org/10.5281/zenodo.6379581.

Goudarouli, Eirini. 2023. 'Digital Innovation and Archival Thinking'. In *Archives: Power, Truth, and Fiction*, edited by Andrew Prescott and Alison Wiggins, 267–81. Oxford: Oxford University Press. https://doi.org/10.1093/oxfordhb/9780198829324.013.0019.

Goudarouli, Eirini, Valentina Vavassori, Jane Winters, Isobel Akerman, Enaiê Azambuja, James Baker, David Beavan et al. 2023. 'Archives and the Environment Report'. https://doi.org/10.5281/zenodo.10066510.

Graban, Tarez Samra, Paul Marty, Allen Romano and Micah Vandegrift. 2019. 'Introduction: Questioning Collaboration, Labor, and Visibility in Digital Humanities Research'. *Digital Humanities Quarterly* 13 (2). Accessed 16 December 2025. https://www.digitalhumanities.org/dhq/vol/13/2/000416/000416.html.

The Guardian. 2017. '"Tsunami of Data" Could Consume One Fifth of Global Electricity by 2025'. *The Guardian*, 11 December 2017, sec. Environment. Accessed 16 December 2025. https://www.theguardian.com/environment/2017/dec/11/tsunami-of-data-could-consume-fifth-global-electricity-by-2025.

Hall, Stuart. 1999. 'Whose Heritage? Un-settling "the Heritage", Re-imagining the Post-nation'. *Third Text* 13 (49): 3–13. https://doi.org/10.1080/09528829908576818.

Hamilton, Gill and Fred Saunderson. 2017. *Open Licensing for Cultural Heritage*. London: Facet Publishing.

Harrison, Rodney, Nélia Dias and Kristian Kristiansen, eds. 2023. *Critical Heritage Studies and the Futures of Europe*. London: UCL Press. Accessed 16 December 2025. https://discovery.ucl.ac.uk/id/eprint/10178909/1/Critical-Heritage-Studies-and-the-Futures-of-Europe.pdf.

Hermon, Sorin and Franco Niccolucci. 2021. 'FAIR Data and Cultural Heritage Special Issue Editorial Note'. *International Journal on Digital Libraries* 22 (3): 251–5. https://doi.org/10.1007/s00799-021-00309-8.

Hern, Alex. 2019. 'Myspace Loses All Content Uploaded before 2016'. *The Guardian*, 18 March 2019, sec. Technology. Accessed 16 December 2025. https://www.theguardian.com/technology/2019/mar/18/myspace-loses-all-content-uploaded-before-2016.

Huang, Patricia H. 2020. 'Managing Digital Image Licensing Services in Art History Museums'. *The Journal of Arts Management, Law, and Society* 50 (4–5): 220–33. https://doi.org/10.1080/10632921.2020.1815615.

Hughes, Lorna M. 2004. *Digitizing Collections. Strategic Issues for the Information Manager*. London: Facet Publishing.

Hughes, Lorna M., ed. 2012. *Evaluating and Measuring the Value, Use and Impact of Digital Collections*. London: Facet Publishing.

Ioannides, Marinos, Andreas Georgopoulos and M. Scherer. 2005. 'Standards in Cultural Heritage: The Missing Grammar for the Digital Documentation of the Past'. Turin, Italy. Accessed 16 December 2025. https://www.cipaheritagedocumentation.org/wp-content/uploads/2018/12/Ioannides-e.a.-Standards-in-cultural-heritage_the-missing-grammar-for-the-digital-documentation-of-the-past.pdf.

Jaillant, Lise, ed. 2022. *Archives, Access and Artificial Intelligence Working with Born-Digital and Digitized Archival Collections*. Bielefeld: Transcript Verlag. Accessed 16 December 2025. https://www.transcript-publishing.com/978-3-8376-5584-1/archives-access-and-artificial-intelligence/.

Jensen, Helle Strandgaard. 2021. 'Digital Archival Literacy for (All) Historians'. *Media History* 27 (2): 251–65. https://doi.org/10.1080/13688804.2020.1779047.

Jisc. 2005. 'Digitisation in the UK: The Case for a UK Framework'. Accessed 24 November 2025. https://www.rluk.ac.uk/wp-content/uploads/2014/02/Digitisation_in_the_UK.pdf.

Jisc. 2009. 'Success or Failure of a Digitisation Programme (NOF): Some Evidence'. *Digital Collections* (blog). 11 March 2009. Accessed 16 December 2025. https://digitisation.jiscinvolve.org/wp/2009 /03/11/success-or-failure-of-a-digitisation-programme-nof-some -evidence/.

Jisc. 2024. 'Historical Texts: News'. 13 May 2024. Accessed 16 December 2025. https://web.archive.org/web/20240513075051 /https://historicaltexts.jisc.ac.uk/news#2024-02-29.

Jones, Ed and Michele Seikel, eds. 2016. *Linked Data for Cultural Heritage*. London: Facet Publishing.

Jowitt, Tom. 2017. 'Tales in Tech History: Friends Reunited'. Silicon UK. 26 October 2017. Accessed 16 December 2025. https://www.silicon .co.uk/e-marketing/socialmedia/tales-tech-history-friends-reunited -223969.

Kahn, R. and R. Simon. 2023. 'Skulls, Skin and Names: The Ethics of Managing Heritage Collections Data Online'. In *Can't Touch This: Digital Approaches to Materiality in Cultural Heritage*, edited by Chiara Palladino and Gabriel Bodard, 205–24. London: Ubiquity Press. https: //doi.org/10.5334/bcv.k.

Kamposiori, Christina. 2020. 'Measuring the Impact of Special Collections and Archives in the Digital Age: Opportunities and Challenges'. *LIBER Quarterly: The Journal of the Association of European Research Libraries* 30 (1): 1–31. https://doi.org/10.18352/lq.10345.

Kelly, Brian, Alastair Dunning, Marieke Guy and Lawrie Phipps. n.d. 'Ideology or Pragmatism? Open Standards and Cultural Heritage Web Sites'. Accessed 24 September 2024. https://www.ukoln.ac.uk/qa -focus/documents/papers/ichim03/.

Kitcher, Natasha, Geoff Belknap, Daniel Belteki and Kaspar Beelen. 2026. 'Computer Vision Questions: What Linkage Through Visual Terms Empowers Historians and Curators to Consider'. In *Emergent Histories: New Work in the Digital History of Industry and Collections from the Congruence Engine Project,* edited by Tim Boon and Alexandra Rose. London: UCL Press.

Kizhner, Inna, Melissa Terras, Maxim Rumyantsev, Valentina Khokhlova, Elisaveta Demeshkova, Ivan Rudov and Julia Afanasieva. 2021. 'Digital Cultural Colonialism: Measuring Bias in Aggregated Digitized Content Held in Google Arts and Culture'. *Digital Scholarship in the Humanities* 36 (3): 607–40. https://doi.org/10.1093/llc/fqaa055.

Klamer, Arjo. 2013. 'The Values of Cultural Heritage'. In *Handbook on the Economics of Cultural Heritage*, edited by Ilde Rizzo and Anna Mignosa, 421–37. Cheltenham: Edward Elgar Publishing.

Koerbin, Paul. 2017. 'Revisiting the World Wide Web as Artefact: Case Studies in Archiving Small Data for the National Library of Australia's PANDORA Archive'. In *Web 25: Histories from the First 25 Years of the World Wide Web* edited by Niels Brügger, 191–206. Bern: Peter Lang.

Koster, Lukas and Saskia Woutersen-Windhouwer. 2018. 'FAIR Principles for Library, Archive and Museum Collections: A Proposal for Standards for Reusable Collections'. *The Code4Lib Journal* 40 (May). Accessed 16 December 2025. https://journal.code4lib.org /articles/13427.

Lee, Benjamin C. G. 2023. 'The Collections as "ML Data" Checklist for Machine Learning and Cultural Heritage'. *Journal of the Association for Information Science and Technology.* https://doi.org/10.1002/asi.24765.

Liarokapis, Fotis, Athanasios Voulodimos, Nikolaos Doulamis and Anastasios Doulamis, eds. 2020. *Visual Computing for Cultural Heritage*. Springer Series on Cultural Computing. Cham: Springer International Publishing. https://doi.org/10.1007/978-3-030 -37191-3.

Lusenet, Yola de. 2007. 'Tending the Garden or Harvesting the Fields: Digital Preservation and the UNESCO Charter on the Preservation of the Digital Heritage'. *Library Trends* 56 (1): 164–82.

Luthra, Mrinalini and Maria Eskevich. 2024. 'Data-Envelopes for Cultural Heritage: Going beyond Datasheets'. In *Proceedings of the Workshop on Legal and Ethical Issues in Human Language Technologies* edited by I. Siegert and K. Choukri, 52–65. Torino: ELRA Language Resources Association *2024*.

Mahey, Mahendra, Aisha Al-Abdulla, Sarah Ames, Paula Bray, Gustavo Candela, Sally Chambers, Caleb Derven et al. 2019. *Open a GLAM Lab*. Doha: Digital Cultural Heritage Innovation Labs. Accessed 16 December 2025. https://glamlabs.pubpub.org.

Marcum, Deanna and Roger C. Schonfeld. 2021. *Along Came Google*. Princeton, NJ: Princeton University Press.

Martinez, Merisa and Melissa Terras. 2019. '"Not Adopted": The UK Orphan Works Licensing Scheme and How the Crisis of Copyright in the Cultural Heritage Sector Restricts Access to Digital Content'. *Open Library of Humanities* 5 (1): 36. https://doi.org/10.16995/olh.335.

Max-Planck-Gesellschaft. 2003. 'Berlin Declaration on Open Access to Knowledge in the Sciences and Humanities'. Accessed 16 December 2025. https://openaccess.mpg.de/Berlin-Declaration.

McCrary, Quincy. 2011. 'The Political Nature of Digital Cultural Heritage'. *LIBER Quarterly: The Journal of the Association of European Research Libraries* 20 (3–4): 357–68. https://doi.org/10.18352/lq.8000.

McKenna, Fattori, Joanna Rivera-Carlisle, Alexander Gould, Mia Gabriel Foale, Hannah Andrews and Aurora Hawcroft. 2025. *Heritage Futures: Digital Cultural Heritage as a Site of Imagination, Innovation and Opportunity*. With Hannah Andrew, Stephanie Grant, Aurora Hawcroft, Daniel Head and Ian Thomas. British Council. https://doi.org/10.57884/H3DV-7Q98.

Milligan, Ian. 2015. 'Web Archive Legal Deposit: A Double-Edged Sword'. *Ian Milligan* (blog). 14 July 2015. Accessed 16 December 2025. https://ianmilli.wordpress.com/2015/07/14/web-archive-legal-deposit-a-double-edged-sword/.

Milligan, Ian. 2024. *Averting the Digital Dark Age: How Archivists, Librarians and Technologists Built the Web a Memory*. Baltimore: Johns Hopkins University Press, 1.

Ministère de l'Enseignement supérieur et de la Recherche. 2024. 'France 2030: 6 projets lauréats du dispositif "programmes de recherche en sciences humaines et sociales"'. Accessed 16 December 2025. https://www.enseignementsup-recherche.gouv.fr/fr/france-2030-6-projets-laureats-du-dispositif-programmes-de-recherche-en-sciences-humaines-et-98168.

Münster, S., F. I. Apollonio, P. Bell, P. Kuroczynski, I. Di Lenardo, F. Rinaudo and R. Tamborrino. 2019. 'Digital Cultural Heritage Meets Digital Humanities'. *The International Archives of the Photogrammetry, Remote Sensing and Spatial Information Sciences* XLII-2/W15 (August): 813–20. https://doi.org/10.5194/isprs-archives-XLII-2-W15-813-2019.

Museum Data Service. n.d. 'About'. Accessed 24 September 2024. https://museumdata.uk/about/.

The National Archives of the UK. 2016. 'The Application of Technology Assisted Review to Born-Digital Records Transfer, Inquiries and Beyond'. Accessed 16 December 2025. https://cdn.nationalarchives

.gov.uk/documents/technology-assisted-review-to-born-digital
-records-transfer.pdf.

National Library of the Netherlands. n.d. 'Statement on Commercial
Generative AI'. Accessed 17 September 2024. https://www.kb.nl/en
/ai-statement.

Neudecker, Clemens. 2022. 'Cultural Heritage as Data: Digital Curation
and Artificial Intelligence in Libraries'. In *CEUR Workshop Proceedings
Qurator 2022: 3rd Conference on Digital Curation Technologies,
September 19–23, 2022, Berlin, Germany*. Accessed 16 December 2025.
https://ceur-ws.org/Vol-3234/paper2.pdf.

The Nightshade Team. n.d. 'Nightshade: Protecting Copyright'.
Accessed 17 September 2024. https://nightshade.cs.uchicago.edu
/whatis.html.

Nora, Pierre. 1989. 'Between Memory and History: Les Lieux de
Mémoire'. *Representations* 26: 7–24. https://doi.org/10.2307/2928520.

Nowviskie, Bethany. 2012. 'Evaluating Collaborative Digital Scholarship
(or, Where Credit Is Due)'. *Journal of Digital Humanities* 4 (1). Accessed
16 December 2025. https://journalofdigitalhumanities.org/1-4
/evaluating-collaborative-digital-scholarship-by-bethany-nowviskie/.

OpenGLAM. n.d.-a. Accessed 16 December 2025. https://openglam.org/.

OpenGLAM. n.d.-b. 'OpenGLAM Principles'. Accessed 31 January 2025.
https://openglam.org/principles/.

Ortolja-Baird, Alexandra and Julianne Nyhan. 2022. 'Encoding the
Haunting of an Object Catalogue: On the Potential of Digital
Technologies to Perpetuate or Subvert the Silence and Bias of the
Early-Modern Archive'. *Digital Scholarship in the Humanities* 37 (3):
844–67. https://doi.org/10.1093/llc/fqab065.

Owens, Trevor and Thomas Padilla. 2021. 'Digital Sources and Digital
Archives: Historical Evidence in the Digital Age'. *International Journal
of Digital Humanities* 1 (3): 325–41. https://doi.org/10.1007/s42803
-020-00028-7.

Padilla, T. G. 2018. 'Collections as Data: Implications for Enclosure'.
College and Research Libraries News 79 (6): 296–300. http://dx.doi.org
/10.5860/crln.79.6.296.

Padilla, Thomas. 2019. 'Responsible Operations: Data Science, Machine
Learning, and AI in Libraries'. Dublin, OH: OCLC Research. https://doi
.org/10.25333/xk7z-9g97.

Padilla, Thomas, Laurie Allen, Hannah Frost, Sarah Potvin, Elizabeth Russey Roke and Stewart Varner. 2019. 'Always Already Computational: Collections as Data'. https://doi.org/10.5281/zenodo.3152935.

Padilla, Thomas, Hannah Scates Kettler and Yasmeen Shorish. 2023. 'Collections as Data: Part to Whole Final Report (Version 1)'. https://doi.org/10.5281/zenodo.10161976.

Pendergrass, Keith, Walker Sampson, Tim Walsh and Laura Alagna. 2019. 'Toward Environmentally Sustainable Digital Preservation'. *The American Archivist* 82 (1): 165–206. https://doi.org/10.17723/0360 -9081-82.1.165.

Pennock, Maureen. 2013. 'Web-Archiving'. Digital Preservation Coalition. https://doi.org/10.7207/twr13-01.

Popple, Simon, Andrew Prescott and Daniel Mutibwa, eds. 2020. *Communities, Archives and New Collaborative Practices*. Bristol: Policy Press.

Prażmowska, Karolina. 2020. 'Misappropriation of Indigenous Cultural Heritage: Intellectual Property Rights in the Digital Era'. *Santander Art and Culture Law Review* 2 (6): 119–50.

Prescott, Andrew and Alison Wiggins. 2024. *Archives: Power, Truth, and Fiction*. Oxford: Oxford University Press.

Rees, Arran John. 2021. 'Remixing Museology: An Approach to Collecting Social Media in Museums'. PhD thesis, University of Leeds. Accessed 16 December 2025. https://etheses.whiterose.ac.uk/29542/.

Rhizome. n.d. 'The Making of Rhizome's Net Art Anthology: Eduardo Kac's Reabracadabra'. Google Arts & Culture. Accessed 26 September 2024. https://artsandculture.google.com/story /the-making-of-rhizome-s-net-art-anthology-eduardo-kac-s -reabracadabra/0gWRpxLUkktNKA.

Richardson, Lorna-Jane. 2022. 'The Dark Side of Digital Heritage: Ethics and Sustainability in Digital Practice'. In *Critical Archaeology in the Digital Age: Proceedings of the 12th IEMA Visiting Scholars Conference*, edited by Kevin Gartski, 201–10. Los Angeles, CA: Cotsen Institute of Archaeology Press.

Ridge, Mia, Samantha Blickhan, Meghan Ferriter et al. 2021. *The Collective Wisdom Handbook: Perspectives on Crowdsourcing in Cultural Heritage*. Accessed 16 December 2025. https://britishlibrary .pubpub.org/.

Rijksmuseum. n.d. 'Open Data Policy: Rijksmuseum'. Accessed 16 December 2025. https://www.rijksmuseum.nl/en/research /conduct-research/data/policy.

Risam, Roopika. 2018. 'Decolonizing the Digital Humanities in Theory and Practice'. In *The Routledge Companion to Media Studies and Digital Humanities*, edited by Jentery Sayers, 78–86. New York: Routledge. https://doi.org/10.4324/9781315730479-8.

Rivero, Athena Chapekis, Samuel Bestvater, Emma Remy and Gonzalo Rivero. 2024. 'When Online Content Disappears'. *Pew Research Center* (blog). 17 May 2024. Accessed 16 December 2025. https: //www.pewresearch.org/data-labs/2024/05/17/when-online-content -disappears/.

Rizzo, Ilde and Anna Mignosa. 2013. *Handbook on the Economics of Cultural Heritage*. Cheltenham: Edward Elgar Publishing, xxiv.

Rouhani, Bijan. 2025. *Digital Heritage and the Global South: Ethics, Politics, and Futures: Concept Note for the Digital Heritage and the Global South Conference*. 3 June 2025. https://doi.org/10.5281 /zenodo.15584527.

Rutherford, Ananda, Anna-Maria Sichani, Katrina Foxton and Sara Perry. 2024. 'Ethics as Practice: Report on the 1st Discovery Project Ethics Workshop'. Towards a National Collection. https://doi.org/10.5281 /zenodo.13683142.

Samaroudi, Myrsini, Karina Rodriguez Echavarria and Lara Perry. 2020. 'Heritage in Lockdown: Digital Provision of Memory Institutions in the UK and US of America during the COVID-19 Pandemic'. *Museum Management and Curatorship* 35 (4): 20–21, 337–61. https://doi.org/10 .1080/09647775.2020.1810483.

Schafer, Valérie and Fred Pailler. 2024. '"All Your Image Are Belong to Us": Heritagization, Archiving and Historicization of Memes'. *Visual Communication* 23 (3): 527–43. https://doi.org/10.1177 /14703572231221030.

Schafer, Valérie and Jane Winters. 2021. 'The Values of Web Archives'. *International Journal of Digital Humanities* 2 (1): 129–44. https://doi .org/10.1007/s42803-021-00037-0.

Schorlemer, Sabine von. 2020. 'UNESCO and the Challenge of Preserving the Digital Cultural Heritage'. *Santander Art and Culture Law Review* 6 (2): 33–64.

Sever, Hande. 2020. 'Biases within Digital Repositories: The Getty Research Portal'. *Stedelijk Studies Journal* 1 (January). https://doi.org/10.54533/StedStud.vol010.art03.

Sherratt, Tim. 2021. 'The GLAM Workbench: A Labs Approach?' 15 June 2021. https://doi.org/10.5281/zenodo.5121188.

Sichani, Anna-Maria. 2022. 'Embracing Decline in Digital Scholarship beyond Sustainability'. In *The Bloomsbury Handbook to the Digital Humanities*, edited by James O'Sullivan, 317–24. London: Bloomsbury Publishing.

Smith, Laurajane. 2006. *Uses of Heritage*. Abingdon: Taylor & Francis.

Smithies, James, Carina Westling, Anna-Maria Sichani, Pam Mellen and Arianna Ciula. 2019. 'Managing 100 Digital Humanities Projects: Digital Scholarship & Archiving in King's Digital Lab'. *Digital Humanities Quarterly* 13 (1): para 20. Accessed 16 December 2025. https://dhq.digitalhumanities.org/vol/13/1/000411/000411.html.

SNARC | Semantic Name Authority Repository Cymru. n.d. 'Main Page'. Accessed 9 October 2024. https://snarc-llgc.wikibase.cloud/wiki/Main_Page.

Somers, James. 2017. 'Torching the Modern-Day Library of Alexandria'. *The Atlantic* (blog). 20 April 2017. Accessed 25 December 2025. https://www.theatlantic.com/technology/archive/2017/04/the-tragedy-of-google-books/523320/.

Speakman, Robert, Mark Michael Hall and David Walsh. 2018. 'User Engagement with Generous Interfaces for Digital Cultural Heritage'. In *Digital Libraries for Open Knowledge*, edited by Eva Méndez, Fabio Crestani, Cristina Ribeiro, Gabriel David and João Correia Lopes, 11057: 186–91. Lecture Notes in Computer Science. Cham: Springer International Publishing. https://doi.org/10.1007/978-3-030-00066-0_16.

Stokel-Walker, Chris. 2023. 'TechScape: Why Twitter Ending Free Access to Its APIs Should Be a "Wake-up Call"'. *The Guardian*, 7 February 2023, sec. Technology. Accessed 16 December 2025. https://www.theguardian.com/technology/2023/feb/07/techscape-elon-musk-twitter-api.

Tanha, Jafar, Veronica Romero and Jesse de Does. 2013. 'tranScriptorium: Tools for Development and Deployment of Linguistic Resources for HTR'. Accessed 16 December 2025. https://www.researchgate.net/publication/260157072_D4_1_Tools_for_development_and_deployment_of_linguistic_resources_for_HTR.

Tanner, Simon. 2012. 'Measuring the Impact of Digital Resources: The Balanced Value Impact Model'. Accessed 16 December 2025. https://kclpure.kcl.ac.uk/ws/portalfiles/portal/5675881 /BalancedValueImpactModel_SimonTanner_October2012.pdf.

Tasovac, Toma, Sally Chambers and Erzsébet Tóth-Czifra. 2020. 'Cultural Heritage Data from a Humanities Research Perspective: A DARIAH Position Paper'. Accessed 16 December 2025. https://hal.science/hal -02961317v1.

Terras, Melissa. 2015. 'Opening Access to Collections: The Making and Using of Open Digitised Cultural Content'. *Online Information Review* 39 (5). https://doi.org/10.1108/OIR-06-2015-0193.

Terras, Melissa. 2022. 'Digital Humanities and Digitised Cultural Heritage'. In *The Bloomsbury Handbook to the Digital Humanities*, edited by James O'Sullivan, 255–66. London: Bloomsbury. https: //doi.org/10.5040/9781350232143.ch-24.

Terras, Melissa, Stephen Coleman, Steven Drost, Chris Elsden, Ingi Helgason, Susan Lechelt, Nicola Osborne et al. 2021. 'The Value of Mass-Digitised Cultural Heritage Content in Creative Contexts'. *Big Data & Society* 8 (1): 2. https://doi.org/10.1177/20539517211006165.

Thylstrup, Nanna Bonde. 2019. *The Politics of Mass Digitization*. Cambridge, MA: MIT Press, 4.

Tucker, Joanna. 2022. 'Facing the Challenge of Digital Sustainability as Humanities Researchers'. *Journal of the British Academy* 10: 93–120. https://doi.org/10.5871/jba/010.093.

UNESCO, 2009. 'Charter on the Preservation of the Digital Heritage: Article 1 – Scope. Accessed 16 December 2025. https: //unesdoc.unesco.org/ark:/48223/pf0000179529.

Uzelac, Aleksandra and Barbara Lovrinić Higgins. 2025. 'From Data to Impact: Assessing the Value of Cultural Heritage in the Digital Age'. *Heritage* 8 (4): 12, 117. https://doi.org/10.3390/heritage8040117.

Valeonti, Foteini, Melissa Terras and Andrew Hudson-Smith. 2020. 'How Open Is Open GLAM? Identifying Barriers to Commercial and Non-Commercial Reuse of Digitised Art Images'. *Journal of Documentation* 76 (1): 1–26. https://doi.org/10.1108/JD-06-2019-0109.

Vasileva, Saiyyna and Nicole McNeilly. 2024. 'Measuring the Instances and Value of Digital Cultural Heritage Reuse'. Europeana Foundation. Accessed 16 December 2025. https://pro.europeana.eu/post /measuring-the-impact-of-reuse-of-digital-heritage.

Villaespesa, Elena, Madhav Tankha, Alejandra Estigarribia, Kate Nadel and Elena Korshakova. 2021. 'Evaluating the Usability of Museum APIs'. Center for Digital Experiences. Accessed 16 December 2025. https://prattdx.org/research/evaluating-the-usability-of -museum-apis/.

Wallace, Andrea. 2022a. 'A Culture of Copyright: A Scoping Study on Open Access to Digital Cultural Heritage Collections in the UK'. Report commissioned by the Towards a National Collection pro- gramme. https://dx.doi.org/10.2139/ssrn.4323683.

Wallace, Andrea. 2022b. 'Surrogate Intellectual Property Rights in the Cultural Sector'. *Journal of Law, Technology and Policy* 303. Accessed 16 December 2025. https://papers.ssrn.com/sol3/papers.cfm ?abstract_id=4323691.

Wallace, Andrea and Ellen Euler. 2020. 'Revisiting Access to Cultural Heritage in the Public Domain: EU and International Developments'. *International Review of Intellectual Property and Competition Law* 51: 823–55. http://dx.doi.org/10.2139/ssrn.3575772.

Wallenius, Anni. 2022. 'Collecting Social Photo: A Nordic Project in the Search of Sustainable Methods for Preserving Social Media as Cultural Heritage'. In *Documentation as Art: Expanded Digital Practices*, edited by Annet Dekker and Gabriella Giannachi, 158–71. Abingdon: Routledge.

Walters Art Museum. 2011. 'The Walters Art Museum Removes Copyright Restrictions from More than 10,000 Images'. 4 October. Accessed 24 November 2025. https://thewalters.org/news/removes-copyright/.

Webb, Sharon. 2018. 'Preserving Community Archives'. Accessed 24 November 2025. https://preservingcommunityarchives.co.uk/.

Wilkinson, Mark D., Michel Dumontier, IJsbrand Jan Aalbersberg, Gabrielle Appleton, Myles Axton, Arie Baak, Niklas Blomberg et al. 2016. 'The FAIR Guiding Principles for Scientific Data Management and Stewardship'. *Scientific Data* 3 (1): 160018. https://doi.org/10 .1038/sdata.2016.18.

Wilson, Daniel C. S. 2022. 'Working at Scale: What Do Computational Methods Mean for Research Using Cases, Models and Collections?' *Science Museum Group Journal*. https://dx.doi.org/10 .15180/221805.

Winters, Jane. 2020. 'Giving with One Click, Taking with the Other: Electronic Legal Deposit, Web Archives and Researcher Access'. In

Electronic Legal Deposit: Shaping the Library Collections of the Future, edited by Paul Gooding and Melissa Terras, 159–78. London: Facet Publishing.

Winters, Jane, John Stack, Kalyan Dutia, Jamie Unwin, Rhiannon Lewis, Richard Palmer and Angela Wolff. 2022. 'Heritage Connector: A Towards a National Collection Foundation Project Final Report'. https://doi.org/10.5281/zenodo.6022678.

Woodhouse, Susi. 2001. 'The People's Network and the Learning Revolution: Building the NOF Digitize Programme'. *Ariadne* 29. Accessed 16 December 2025. https://www.ariadne.ac.uk/issue/29/woodhouse/.

Wright, William C. C. and Florian V. Eppink. 2016. 'Drivers of Heritage Value: A Meta-Analysis of Monetary Valuation Studies of Cultural Heritage'. *Ecological Economics* 130 (October): 277–84. https://doi.org/10.1016/j.ecolecon.2016.08.001.

Zaagsma, Gerben. 2023. 'Digital History and the Politics of Digitization'. *Digital Scholarship in the Humanities* 38 (2): 830–51. https://doi.org/10.1093/llc/fqac050.

Zuanni, Chiara. 2023. 'Object Biographies in the Digital Age: Documentation, Life-Histories, and Data'. *International Journal of Heritage Studies* 29 (7): 695–710. https://doi.org/10.1080/13527258.2023.2215733.

Index